# Queer and Trans Artists of Color:
## Stories of Some of Our Lives

### Interviews by Nia King

### Co-edited by Jessica Glennon-Zukoff and Terra Mikalson

Queer and Trans Artists of Color: Stories of Some of Our Lives
Copyright © 2014 by Nia King
All rights reserved.
ISBN: 1492215643
ISBN-13: 978-1492215646

# Table of Contents

Foreword by Toi Scott.................................................................i
Introduction by Nia King..........................................................v

## Interviews

Ryka Aoki ................................................................................1
Van Binfa.................................................................................17
Micia Mosely...........................................................................29
Yosimar Reyes.........................................................................45
Kortney Ryan Ziegler..............................................................61
Lovemme Corazón..................................................................69
Fabian Romero........................................................................87
Magnoliah Black.....................................................................103
Kiam Marcelo Junio................................................................117
Miss Persia and Daddie$ Pla$tik.............................................125
Virgie Tovar............................................................................141
Julio Salgado...........................................................................155
Nick Mwaluko........................................................................169
Leah Lakshmi Piepzna-Samarsinha.........................................185
Janet Mock..............................................................................195
Nia King..................................................................................211

## Bios

Artist bios................................................................................221
Editor bios...............................................................................226

Acknowledgements.................................................................229

**Foreword**
by Toi Scott

I remember the first time I heard the acronym that would change my life forever: QTPOC[1], short for queer and transgender people of color. I was embarrassed to ask what it stood for at first, but it quickly became an integral part of my identity. It helped me discover the safe spaces my peers and predecessors had meticulously carved out over the decades. Safe. Brown. Queer. Spaces. Spaces where I felt seen, protected, and appreciated for who I was. Spaces that freed me to discover myself and define myself as an activist, and more importantly, as an *art* activist.

Gathering and sharing our stories—expressing our voices through art—is and always has been necessary for queer and trans people of color's survival. Since the cultural theft that took place during colonization and slavery, people of color have had the immense task of resisting invisibility, assimilation, and erasure. This is particularly true for queer and trans people of color because violently eliminating gender and sexual diversity was an integral part of the colonization process in many countries.

Queer and trans people of color's contributions continue to be erased within art and social movements, though we have often been at the forefront of movements for social change. For example, gay Black civil rights leader Bayard Rustin, a mentor and advisor to Martin Luther King, Jr., was a leading strategist for the civil rights movement and chief organizer of the 1963 March on Washington for Jobs and Freedom, but he is rarely mentioned in history books.

---

[1] Nia's note: QTPOC is pronounced "QT" like "cutie" and "POC" as in Tupac.

Queer and transgender people of color have often been relegated to the margins of straight communities of color and white queer communities, or experienced welcoming only under the condition that we left our difference at the door. Increasingly, queer and trans people of color are carving out spaces that center our experiences, both in art and in the real world. By sharing our stories and knowledge we prove we exist, thus combating the erasure of queer people of color from queer history and from the history of struggles for racial justice in the US.

Like Langston Hughes, Zora Neale Hurston, and other contributors to FIRE! (one of the first Black queer independent publications) during the Harlem Renaissance, we find ourselves having to create our own cultural institutions in order to have our voices heard. Like Sylvia Rivera, Marsha P. Johnson, and their sisters at Street Transvestite Action Revolutionaries (STAR) who were part of the Gay Liberation Front, our narratives exist in opposition to white queer assimilationist agendas. We stand on the shoulders of queer ancestors like James Baldwin, Audre Lorde, and Gloria E. Anzaldúa who used their voices to write against erasure and the historical forgetting of queer people of color's vital struggle.

**Necessity of Documenting and Sharing Our Stories**

Nia King has passionately sought to archive the experiences of queer and trans people of color who are committed to art as a tool for political change. Her work with QTPOC artists on her podcast "We Want the Airwaves" is an important and innovative contribution to the oral history record, not just for queer and trans people of color, but for everyone.

So often in the media, others tell our stories from their perspectives, taking liberties and making assumptions and omissions, many times without our knowledge or consent. Nia shifts this dynamic by documenting the stories of the marginalized in their own words. She takes on the important task of curating those experiences, and recognizes the inherent power and healing in QTPOC artists being able to tell their own stories without having to self-censor for the sake of straight white audiences. Nia highlights artists who are using art as a tool for affirming and uncovering our community's innate power.

**Solidarity in Storytelling**

It is important that we see this book as an act of solidarity among different groups that fall under the acronym QTPOC. It is revolutionary that this book provides a space where our stories of struggle, survival, celebration, and success are placed side by side, where we can truly begin to understand each other's experiences and value our cultural and political differences.

It can be healing to share stories within QTPOC communities, because our experiences of racism, homophobia, and transphobia are often silenced and invalidated in the outside world. QTPOC storytellers can find affirmation and legitimacy in sharing stories with those whose experiences echo their own. For QTPOC audience members, witnessing a story that resonates with them lets them know that they are not alone and that the challenges they face are not imagined.

**Survival: One Story at a Time**

Seeds of survival exist within liberatory art that helps us see the unseen and speak the unspoken. Art can raise awareness about oppression, move people to action, and help us envision the better world we are working towards.

For queer and trans people of color, art isn't frivolous upper-class entertainment. Our writing, performances, and visual art are in keeping with the tradition of our predecessors who used stories to share knowledge, heal trauma, and envision liberation. The brave, brilliant, beautiful spirits who bare their souls in this book do so as an act of love, healing, and solidarity. Their stories break free from the shadows so that our existence may be visible. Nia King and the artists featured in *Queer and Trans Artists of Color: Stories of Some of Our Lives* have given our QTPOC community the invaluable gift of voice and remembrance. The silence has been broken. We will not be forgotten y la lucha sigue.

Love, Healing, and Solidarity,

Toi Scott

# Introduction

In 2012, when I interviewed to be a New Media and Communications Intern at Colorlines.com, my future boss Channing Kennedy said to me, "What is it that you really want to be doing?"

"I want to be an artist for the movement," I replied.

"Then why aren't you making art?" he asked.

So I picked up a pencil to draw again for the first time in years.

I didn't think it was possible for people to make a living off of their art, especially not queer brown people. Trying to make a living as an artist seemed hard enough without racism and homophobia working against you. In 2013 I set out to interview artists who were "like me," in that they were queer people of color, but "unlike me" in that they were successful. I started a podcast called "We Want the Airwaves" to share their stories and strategies for "making it" in the art world.

My heroes have always been storytellers, and storytelling takes many forms. Included in this collection of interviews are poets and writers—such as Ryka Aoki, Yosimar Reyes, and Fabian Romero—who might be considered more traditional storytellers by virtue of their medium, but there are also musicians (Daddie$ Pla$tik), a drag queen (Miss Persia), a burlesque performer (Magnoliah Black), and a stand-up comic (Micia Mosely). All of these artists practice forms of storytelling that are meant to be accessible and tell stories that carry a political message, whether it's insisting on the right to remain in the increasingly unaffordable city of San Francisco (like Miss Persia and Daddie$ Pla$tik) or that fat Black bodies are beautiful (like Magnoliah Black).

Not all of the artists featured in this book and on "We Want the Airwaves" are performers. The book also includes visual artists such as cartoonist Van Binfa and illustrator Julio Salgado. As much as I love performance, as an introvert, I secretly really identify with these behind-the-scenes people.

So what happened behind the scenes of the podcast that resulted in this book? To produce the podcast, I book guests, research their work, prepare questions, interview them, edit the audio, record an introduction, add music, run the edited interview by the artists for approval, make any changes they request, and then convert and upload the audio files to my website, artactivistnia.com.

I also had all podcast interviews transcribed so that the content would be accessible to deaf and hard-of-hearing audiences. I didn't feel comfortable asking people to do the transcription work for free, so I raised money online through IndieGoGo to be able to pay transcribers. Once I had invested money into interview transcriptions, it occurred to me that I could turn the podcast into a book. It had also come to my attention that a lot of people (my parents, for example) didn't listen to podcasts, were unlikely to access the transcripts online, and thus were missing out on this unique archive of stories I was building.

I enlisted the help of my friends Jessica Glennon-Zukoff and Terra Mikalson to co-edit the book. Both are fellow Mills College alums who graduated within a few years of me (Mills is where I met them). Terra was an Ethnic Studies major, and we took several classes together. Jessica was an English Literature and Women's, Gender, and Sexuality Studies double major. I knew both of them to have politics aligned with my own and to pay impeccable attention to detail. Without their hard work, this dream of releasing a collection of my podcast interviews in book form never would have come to fruition.

Jessica and Terra's jobs, perhaps more so than even my own, were behind-the-scenes. When I got the transcripts back from transcribers, they were in rough shape; the way most of us speak in conversation doesn't make for an easy read. Terra and Jessica were charged with spinning straw into gold, making raw transcripts of real conversations (peppered with "ums," "likes," and lots of incomplete sentences) into something clear and blissfully easy to read. I think they knocked it out of the park.

Being an editor/curator is weird. It felt weird to cut artists' words, add words, and change words for clarity when necessary. To mitigate some of this weirdness, each artist was given three opportunities to look at the transcripts and give feedback—one after we did each round of edits—so they could let us know if we had made any mistakes in our attempts to achieve both clarity and flow. Jessica, Terra, the artist, and I all ultimately spent time editing each transcript.

Each of the artists featured in this book is not only making art to empower and affirm the lives of queer and trans people of color—they are also each amazing storytellers. I hope you enjoy Nick Mwaluko's stories about growing up gay in East Africa, Kiam's pre-teen dreams of becoming a pop star, and Lovemme's candid words about why she published her first book at nineteen.

It has been a pleasure to work with each of these artists and both of my co-editors. I am so grateful to those who believed in this project and helped me get it off the ground: the artists, the transcribers, the donors, Terra, Jessica, and many others who are listed individually on the acknowledgments page.

# A word on queer and trans grammar

You may find a few things that look out of the ordinary in some of these interviews. Here's what's behind those choices:

- Van Binfa specifically requested that we use "Latin@" instead of "Latino/a."
- The gender-neutral or genderqueer pronouns "ze" and "hir" can be found in Ryka Aoki's transcript. "Ze" stands in place for "he" or "she" and "hir" stands in place of "him/his" or "her."
- Each of the artists authored their own bio. Lovemme's use of "gurl" instead of "girl" is intentional, as is Janet Mock's spelling of "boss" as "bawse".
- Fabian's pronouns are "they" and "their," so that's how Fabian is referred to in their bio. While "they" is often used to refer to multiple people, it can also be used as a gender-neutral pronoun for a single person.
- Kiam uses both "he" and "they" pronouns for himself, so you will find both in his bio.

You may find a few words in these transcripts that you are not familiar with, although hopefully not too many. "Cisgender" is a word that sometimes throws people. "Cisgender," in short, means "not transgender." Someone who is transgender identifies as a gender other than the one they were assigned at birth; someone who is cisgender identifies with the same gender they were assigned at birth.

## A note on demographics

This collection is a reflection of the intersection of queer and trans artists of color I admire *and* to whom I had access. Thus, most of them are Bay Area-based. I did have the opportunity to interview Fabian Romero of Seattle and Ryka Aoki of Los Angeles when they came to the Bay Area for the National Queer Arts Festival in 2013. I also had the opportunity to interview Van Binfa and Kiam Marcelo Junio when I traveled to Chicago in July of the same year.

No collection of interviews can capture the full diversity of queer and trans communities of color. However, I did my best to interview a wide range of queer and trans people of color with the resources I had available to me. I hope you have the opportunity to see some aspect of your experience reflected within these pages. If you don't, I hope you are inspired to create your own archive or build upon the one that I have created.

Sincerely,

Nia King
ArtActivistNia.com

# Ryka Aoki

**Ryka Aoki:** Nothing in my book *Seasonal Velocities* depended on a handout. Everything was done by trans people, gender-variant people. Anyone who ever touched anything creatively with that book from layout to cover—that entire press was completely trans-run.

I took chances with that book that I would *never* have taken with a straight publisher or a cisgender publisher. It's an honor to be nominated for the Lambda Literary Award. There are some great, great nominees that I'm sharing this with. I hope I win. I hope *we* win. But I think we already did.

**Nia King:** That's a good way to look at it. How do you get on the radar of the Lambda Literary Award committee when you're a small press that has maybe never published a book before? Was this the first book that Trans-Genre Press did?

**Ryka:** Absolutely. You get on their radar by pulling strings. You get on their radar by going to other people's events and learning. When somebody offers you a reading at a time when you know you'll be tired, you take the reading. You take the interview the morning after a show, like we're doing here. Also, I've got an MFA—having letters at the end of my name really, really helps. It matters. It opens doors. Whether or not you think an MFA is a worthwhile thing, when you're broke as an artist, it sure as hell opens doors.

Not everybody who decides who gets the publishing deal is a writer. Some of them are bean counters, some of them are administrators, and they respect—for some odd reason—degrees. Like it or not, that's the game. Like it or not, if you're going to be successful in this country, sooner or later you're going to have to deal with a white man. You just *have* to. Sorry. You may not want it to be this way, but it is.

**Nia:** I think sometimes it's hard to determine the value of something like an MFA. It seems like a lot of times queer folks, trans folks, folks of color really struggle in those spaces of higher education. With all the things you hear about how degrees don't take you as far as they used to, and how there are all these people either unemployed or working jobs that they're way overqualified for, I think sometimes it's hard to know whether it's a worthwhile investment to pursue higher degrees.

**Ryka:** If you're putting yourself through school, I still believe in the MFA. Provided you're willing to *work*. Provided you're willing to stay in when all your friends are out partying. Provided you get up in the morning because you can't stay away from your pen. Provided you can see yourself doing nothing else in the world but writing. *Then* the MFA is an amazing thing. If making art is what you are *born* to do, then the MFA helps *immensely*. You have contacts, you make friends, you learn techniques. If you're going to grad school just to put off the "real world," it doesn't work.

Or if you're *really* tied into street-level community work and that's where you want to be, and you want to work at a community center, and you want to build your life that way, then perhaps leaving the community for school will break your heart. I've seen that happen. I saw people at Cornell University, where I did my MFA, drop out of the program because they couldn't bear to be outside of their community, where there was so much work for them to do.

If you know you belong in an MFA program, an MFA program *will* still help you. If you have any doubts, though—the MFA and the PhD, these programs cost a *lot* of money. I mean, do you want the PhD or do you want the Rolls Royce?

**Nia:** I feel like we still have a ways to go in terms of seeing organizing and art as integrally related, and not having art be something that takes you away from organizing or organizing being something that takes you away from art. I feel like artists like Favianna Rodriguez and Melanie Cervantes are starting to help bridge that gap. What does it look like to be an artist who is also involved in the community and in organizing on the street level?

**Ryka:** I've been blessed with a set of talents. I know what I'm good at and I know what I'm *not* good at. You know, no queer is an island. I write. I can take something and make it sound a little bit better. That is my passion. I think that I depend heavily on the greater community, for everyone to do what they do best.

I think that the political artists, the writers, the filmmakers, and their work provide a lot of thought on that level as well. It's like, "What are we doing here?" It's really too easy to see activism as a succession of battles in the trenches, battles in the trenches, battles in the trenches. And then there's a lot of infighting. I don't know if you know this, but sometimes queers fight each other.

**Nia:** [*laughter*]

**Ryka:** I think a lot of that is wasted effort. I think a lot of that comes from—just in my humble, humble opinion—people thinking they have to sacrifice some of who they are for the greater cause.

Look, I'm a femme—I want it all, baby. Why *can't* I be a poet and have my poetry change the world? Why can't you be a filmmaker and have your films *change* the world? Why can't somebody else be an accountant and have their accounting *change* the world? Why can't somebody else organize a sit-in and have the sit-in *change* the world?

All of these together create that healthier community. We talk about what an organ is. The heart isn't busy breathing, the heart's pumping blood. The kidneys aren't thinking, that's what the brain does. The brain isn't processing air, that's what the lungs do. If we'd just respect each other and trust that we're all doing our job, and are happy doing our job—our passion—I'd be for that.

**Nia:** You started out as a chemist, right? How did you become interested in poetry?

**Ryka:** I have always been interested in poetry. I think it's time I came out—I'm Asian [*laughter*]—and I'm significantly older than you are. There was a time when there weren't very many Asian American writers, and I got not-so-gently shoved into the sciences.

I scored very highly on some of those tests. I'm good at it, but I got shoved in there. I kind of got profiled. If you'd looked at my notebooks from college, the chemistry notes were going from right to left, but if you read left to right, you'd see poetry. I've always wanted to *do* poetry, but I think I kind of bowed to the pressure to be secure at first in my life—to do the safe thing—and it did not work out.

**Nia:** How do you overcome that pressure?

**Ryka:** You almost commit suicide.

**Nia:** [pause] I've been thinking a lot lately about how as I'm interviewing all these super amazing artists, activists, and people who are *so* creative and work *so* hard…a lot of them are broke. A lot of them are really struggling. How do you decide to be an artist when you kind of know that you're never going to make any money? Or *is* it a decision?

**Ryka:** I think that, yes, it is a decision. In fact, I think it *has* to be a decision. It's like being in a relationship. If you fall into the relationship and never quite commit to it, that's completely different than looking at your partner and saying, "Are we in this together? Yes, we're in this together. Really? Forever?" Well, whatever "forever" means to queers…

**Nia:** [*laughter*] I guess my question is how do you let go of the fear of not being able to survive?

**Ryka:** You don't let go of it. You channel it, and you let that fear drive you. Every time that you're afraid, you work harder. You wake up an hour earlier. You don't go out that extra day. You send that email to that person who can help you. You smile. You use that time to think about all the work you need to do. It's weird—when you have that kind of dedication, in turn, your self-talk gets a lot easier to deal with. You don't get away from the fear. You turn the fear around and you let that sucker put you forward.

**Nia:** You think most art is driven by fear?

**Ryka:** I think art is driven by *whatever* emotion it can use. Art is omnivorous. It's important that we be able to channel *all* the emotions. I know artists who only channel hate or who only channel happiness, and what happens if there's nothing more to hate? I try to position myself as an omnivore. If I'm happy, I'm going to write about that. If I'm sad, I'm going to channel that. If I'm pissed off, I'm going to channel that. Fear is just another emotion to channel.

**Nia:** I know your press is called "Trans-Genre," but *Seasonal Velocities* sounds like it really *is* trans-genre, in terms of the different types of writing that are in there.

**Ryka:** Very much so. I divided *Seasonal Velocities* according to seasons, starting with winter and going through fall. In each season, it's almost as if I'm drawing from a different emotion, and I tend to channel different emotions in different ways. There are essays, there are poems, and there are a couple performance pieces. All of these contribute to the collage, so it is very much a mixed-genre book.

When you do a mixed-genre book, you have to be really, really careful because it so easily can just be this pastiche, this collage of just *stuff*. The seasons are, to me, such a primal and inevitable way to organize time—winter, spring, summer, fall. Then, within each chapter, I try to think about the American musical—how songs give emotion to the dialogue, which contextualizes the music, and so on and so forth. I wanted to make sure all my pieces held that way.

**Nia:** Do you feel like pulling from different genres or having a diverse array of mediums you draw from is a political choice?

**Ryka:** I think it's a political artifact. I think that I can't be like Wallace Stevens and go sit in an office somewhere and write poetry for the rest of my life. I don't have a job in the Poetry Department. That's not what I do. There are some times when the immediacy of something is like, "I don't have time to make the metaphor. Here, I'm going to give you an essay." Or "This is a story because I just need to tell it the way it came to me." And then sometimes, "Here's a poem because I really, really need to take the time to break your heart."

In each one of those, you notice it starts with "I need." I think if success had come to me earlier on—in other words, if I hadn't been one of the few people of color in my MFA program or if I hadn't been queer and hadn't been trans, maybe success would have come to me a little bit differently, a little earlier, and I would have found myself ensconced in some poetry department somewhere. At that point, my essays would have seemed more like excursions as opposed to expressions. I think what we're seeing when so many queer and marginalized people do so many different things is a bit of a blessing, but I do think it's also an artifact of oppression.

**Nia:** Yeah. I took a couple of writing classes at Mills College. In both the classes I took, I was one of, I think, *two* people of color in the class, which I imagine is probably not uncommon, but a lot of my writing is about race and I feel like my classmates had a hard time engaging with what I was actually saying. Was that something that you encountered?

**Ryka:** *Absolutely.* At the Cornell program, I was maybe the *second* Asian American in the entire program, *ever*. At the time, we did our copying at the copy center. When I was trying to print handouts for the class for which I was a teaching assistant, the people at the copy center didn't believe I was part of the English Department.

**Nia:** *Wow.*

**Ryka:** I had to get one of my white friends to vouch for me that I was part of the English Department.

**Nia:** *Jesus.* This is when?

**Ryka:** It was the early nineties. When I talked about race or when I just talked about myself, people were like, "Why do you keep bringing race into things?" I was like, "I'm *not* bringing race into things. Can't you see I'm talking about my grandpa, or my grandma, or my *breakfast*? I'm sorry that I'm eating *rice* for breakfast, but I'm not bringing race into it! This is *breakfast* to me!"

*That* part of the MFA experience, when your cohort just doesn't get it, sucks. They can be supportive in so many other ways, but there are these areas where they can't. That's just where you have to think, "I'm in it for myself. I'm here to improve as a writer, to create context, to create community, but in the end, my writing is beholden to me." I hope that helps a little.

**Nia:** Yeah. My friend Nicki Green is a transgender sculptor who does sort of *graphic* work in ceramics, and she was telling me about not being able to get useful feedback or critique on her work *at all* in art school, so she would just bring friends to her critiques so she could actually get useful feedback. Did you have any creative workarounds like that?

**Ryka:** I didn't have friends to do that with. I didn't get much support going into the program, partly because at that particular point in time I'd been working as a chemist, so most of my friends didn't understand why I would give up this really solid job analyzing toxic waste to go write *poetry*.

**Nia:** [*laughter*]

**Ryka:** Oh, boy. There was this one time at my chemistry job when we had oil from a crematorium and I had to analyze flash points. So I'm making *human oil* ignite and I'm just thinking—

**Nia:** [*laughter*]

**Ryka:** "There's got to be a better way! There's just got to be a better way! This oil came from a human being! I can make soap!"

So, anyway—what the hell were we talking about? [*laughter*]

**Nia:** I was asking if you had any creative workarounds for not getting the kind of feedback that would be helpful for your work.

**Ryka:** I think my experience as an abuse victim really helped because you learn what you can and can't expect from your parents. You're not ever going to expect unconditional love—that is just never going to happen—so you're grateful for the food. You're grateful for the good times and you kind of gear up for the bad times. You understand that the shit can hit the fan at *any time*, any place, without warning, so you hoard. I learned how to do that.

When I was in my MFA program, I learned quickly that these people actually had something that I valued: consistency. I knew what kind of criticism I could get, so when they talked about my imagery, I would listen. When they talked about meter, I would listen. When they talked about different forms and other writers I should think about reading, I would listen. But then when they started telling me that I was bringing up race, I would turn it off!

**Nia:** That's really smart. [*laughter*]

**Ryka:** That wisdom came at a price.

**Nia:** So, we talked a little bit about your background as a chemist, making human oil—

**Ryka:** I didn't *make* the human oil! It showed up in a *jar*.

**Nia:** [*laughter*]

**Ryka:** There was this other one that—I didn't always do forensics, but occasionally there'd be, like, this *water* that came from a drowning victim and I'd be shaking this jar thinking, "This is the last thing she ever saw!"

**Nia:** Oh my god. What was your job specifically?

**Ryka:** I was an environmental chemist. With a lot of the stuff, forensics had already passed, and the question was how to dispose of the stuff.

We used to analyze all kinds of things, but sometimes we'd get really good stuff. One time we had to analyze alcohol content for beer, so we all got free beer. It's not always gross stuff.

**Nia:** You're also a master martial artist. What kind of martial arts?

**Ryka:** Judo, although right now I'm teaching a more inclusive form of self-defense, but my background training is judo.

**Nia:** That's cool. I always thought judo was really interesting because you use your opponent's force against them. It's sort of considered a soft form, in that there's not a lot of striking, right?

**Ryka:** No striking in tournament judo whatsoever. I really enjoy judo simply because it's almost like having a conversation. I tell my students, "You don't beat your opponent. You become one with your opponent, and then you master yourself."

**Nia:** That's deep. [*laughter*]

**Ryka:** When I'm in a judo match, it's almost like having a conversation and trying to get my other half to agree with me.

**Nia:** Does that affect or impact the way you look at your social justice work?

**Ryka:** Probably—how could it not? I mean, I've been doing judo since I was *ten*. I was an Asian kid who was a little bit of a bookish geek, had skipped a grade, and was already small anyway. When I started doing judo, by the time I got to green belt, people started leaving me alone.

Whenever there's a fight, there are two types of fighters: the type who wants to show the world they can fight and the type who wants to win. I don't *want* people to know I can fight. The best way for me to win an argument or fight or political battle is to make the other person think they thought of it first. It's just a maneuver. When the person thinks he has thought of it first, he then pursues it with his own passion, so then what I'm actually doing is using his own force against him.

**Nia:** That's so interesting because there are different approaches to social justice and a lot of people feel like anger is a really important, useful tool and that combat is sort of *the* way social justice manifests itself, but it sounds like you have a very different approach. Or maybe this *is* combat—it just looks very different.

**Ryka:** It's *teaching*. I don't see myself as a warrior. I see myself as a teacher. When there's somebody who's my adversary, I don't think of that person as an obstacle. I think of that person as a learning experience. I'm going to sometimes be the student and I'm going to sometimes be the teacher, but we're going to get through this and we're each going to become wiser for the encounter. I'm not a fighter. I love learning. I love teaching. Why can't we use that and have social justice in a way where there doesn't *have* to be a winner or loser, where we *all* become more aware?

**Nia:** Yeah. [*laughter*] I feel like you're describing utopia.

**Ryka:** Yeah, but the person who says, "We're going to kill all our enemies. We're going to be the only ones who are strong and we're going to take justice back"—really? Is that *any* more realistic?

**Nia:** I mean, I don't know if that's justice—

**Ryka:** That's *not* justice. When you hear people going, "We've got to struggle against the man"—to me, that's purgatory. You're going to spend the rest of your life struggling against the man. You dream of purgatory, I'll dream of utopia, and we're still going to work with each other. I'm not going to invalidate you, it's just that I can't see where you're coming from and you can't see where I'm coming from, but you know what? The heart can't see the brain, but they work together.

**Nia:** I really admire and kind of envy your wisdom [*laughter*] and how at peace with all of this you seem.

**Ryka:** I *love* what I do! I *love* to write! I *love* my teaching! You know, I teach on my birthday sometimes and I tell my students, "My birthday wish is for all of you to have a job you love enough that you want to come in on your birthday and do it!"

**Nia:** I'm getting emotional! [*laughter*]

**Ryka:** Aww!

**Nia:** No, that's *really* sweet! You just have this amazing spirit of kindness and generosity. I think it's hard to maintain that. Often, being in social justice struggles makes people jaded and bitter, and you just don't seem to have any of that at all! [*laughter*]

**Ryka:** No. It's like, every day that I can look out and see that tree and see how beautiful the light is off of it, I win.

**Nia:** Yeah. I feel like I look out that window and see the American flag and think about war and nationalism and—

**Ryka:** Sometimes it's good to see the symbols. Sometimes it's good to see the colors. The funny thing about being jaded is that people think that's the end state, that you start from innocence and you become jaded. It's like being a butterfly. You look at the monarch butterfly, and it looks like it's jaded, but actually what's going on under the hard shell is a transformation. I think that if you just stay with the process, eventually you realize this sort of "jaded" covering is simply holding your wings back. Break through it and you'll be fine.

**Nia:** I feel like that's a good place to wrap, unless there's anything else that you'd like to share about yourself or your work?

**Ryka:** I just signed a book deal with Topside Press, so my first novel is going to be coming out.

**Nia:** What kind of press are they?

**Ryka:** They started off as a trans press, but—

**Nia:** Oh, awesome.

**Ryka:** My book that's coming out doesn't have much to do with trans issues. It's pretty much a story based on my family, and I wasn't out as trans at the time. I was at a book panel at the Rainbow Book Fair and I broke down *crying*—on the panel! Not like little tears but [*imitating gasping and sobbing*] that kind of crying. I was talking about my novel *A Hilo Song*, which is about Hilo, a city in Hawai'i. It's on the Big Island and my father's side of the family is there. Many of my best memories come from there. To me, it's the best thing I've ever written, just flat-out, period. I just put every, every, *everything* I had in that book, but there are no trans characters! There are a couple gay characters, but they're very peripheral.

We were talking about trans presses and trans narratives on the panel and all of a sudden I said, "This world keeps telling me that I'm more than trans, that I'm an artist, that everyone's working for me to be a complete human being and blah blah blah. And here I've got this novel that I just think is the most beautiful thing! A couple of my friends have read it and they think it's a great novel, too. But since it's not overtly queer, the very presses that are supposed to support me won't touch this!" I start crying, going, "You say you want me to be complete, but when I'm writing these things, I have to rip my heart in half. What's going on?!"

I think we're at an exciting time right now where people like Tom [Léger, Topside Press publisher], who's just a happy trans guy, kind of realized that in order for this community to grow, we have to not only grow as organizers looking for useful things to keep furthering the queer and trans agenda, but also nurture artists, who are *also* furthering the queer and trans agenda, albeit in a different way.

*Every book I write is trans,* but if we expect our trans people to be *more* than professional trans people, we have to let them be professional chefs, professional doctors. And you know what? When I have my neurologist taking care of *my* brain and ze is a trans or genderqueer person, I don't want that person thinking about hir identity—I want that person thinking about my *brain*!

**Nia:** I think that brings up an interesting point. I went to a workshop recently where people were supposed to get together and talk about race, queerness, and the arts. People were coming from *really* different places. There was someone who was like, "I'm not going to check the 'Asian' box or the 'queer' box to get money. As an artist, I reject labels. If you can't deal with it, then that's your problem."

I've been thinking a lot about whether being a queer artist and/or artist of color is an asset or a liability. I think in some ways it opens a lot of doors. When Black History Month comes around, a lot of Black artists have a chance to show work and make money that maybe they don't the rest of the year. But at the same time, if you're *not* making work about race or about queerness and you're only getting a chance to perform at those kind of themed shows, then what does that mean?

**Ryka:** For me, rule number one is when the white man gives you money, take the money and run. You just won. So you had to check off that you're Asian—you get to pay rent! That's cool. You can do a lot of things with a roof over your head.

What helps get me out of being pigeonholed are the backdoor dealings, talking to people. If one gets pigeonholed on stage, there's no pigeonholing off stage. One can go to whatever show they want, usually. Especially on the West Coast. I just find that being nice and *really* trying to listen to the work goes a long way. Then you start talking to the people, and you start learning a little bit, and instead of breaking the walls down, you look for the door.

I don't handle anger very well, and it's easier for me to believe that if you find the right way in, most people are not assholes.

Transcribed by Weily Lang

## Van Binfa

**Van Binfa:** About two or three years ago, I was constantly searching for somebody like myself. I would go to trans groups and they would be predominantly white. I would go to queer spaces and I would find other Latinos, but they were all cisgender. It was really hard for me to find other trans Latin@s.

My Soy Quien Soy Trans Empowerment Collective [SQS] co-founder Ivonne Canellada and I decided that we were going to fix that and at least do a little something for the trans Latin@ community. We based ourselves in Pilsen [in Chicago's Lower West Side], which was really, really important because a lot of the trans resources and support are in the North Side, which is more accessible to white gay men. We wanted to branch out from there. We started at Efebina's Cafe, doing once-a-month gatherings where we had coffee and talked about doing things. Through SQS, we've done a couple of workshops. We've worked with Howard Brown, Center on Halsted—I mean, we've worked with pretty much anybody in Chicago who's involved with LGBT activism. It has been wonderful. We've done anything from Trans 101 to self-defense workshops.

Soy Quien Soy is on hold for now, as I've been going through personal medical issues this year. I just haven't been able to get down to Pilsen. I think we're going to be shifting into more of an online resource. SQS is pretty much my baby.

**Nia King:** For those of us who might not be familiar with Chicago geography, could you talk a little bit about Pilsen and why it felt important to you for your group to meet there?

**Van:** Pilsen is incredibly queer-friendly. I think a lot of people don't know that because they think, "Oh, my gosh, it's primarily

Latin@s and they're Catholic and super conservative!" But there's a thriving queer community in Pilsen, which is just wonderful to be part of. I didn't want to centralize us in a place where everybody else was already. Any queer person of color who lived more towards the South Side would always have to travel north for queer resources and community events, so I didn't want to continue that trend. I wanted to set SQS apart and start somewhere new.

**Nia:** I went to a queer event called Salon-a-thon last night in Chicago. It was really interesting to see the similarities and differences between queer events that I've been to in the Bay versus here. In my experience, the Bay Area queer community is really segregated, perhaps even more so by gender than by race. You kind of have the queer cis women hanging out together and with the trans male community. There's some overlap because people are dating each other and sometimes have overlapping friend circles, but then the gay cis male community feels totally separate. I don't know if trans women in the Bay have their own separate communities or if they're just forced into the margins of the other communities that exist. It feels different here in Chicago, but I've only been here a week. I'm curious to hear what your thoughts are.

**Van:** I feel like there is that segregation to an extent because Lakeview/Boystown is white, cis, gay male territory.

**Nia:** "Territory" makes them sound like a gang.

**Van:** Yeah, the most fabulous gang ever! [*laughter*] There's just so much problematic shit that goes on in Boystown. There was this whole "Take Back Boystown" campaign. I don't want to say it was like a scandal, but everybody was talking about it. The affluent, white, cis, gay men—part of that "gang"—were trying to push out the queer youth of color who had started coming into Lakeview to access the Center on Halsted or Howard Brown or the Broadway Youth Center—all of these *big*, government-funded resources. It really upset a lot of people. They were like, "Our neighborhood's going to hell. Let's take back Boystown."

**Nia:** Wow. I assumed when you said "Take back Boystown" that you meant *from* the rich, white, gay, cis men.

**Van:** Oh, fuck no! It's expensive to live in Boystown. You have million-dollar apartments in Boystown. They were trying to take back "their" neighborhood, and it started a lot of community discussions about—

**Nia:** Racism? [*laughter*]

**Van:** Yeah! About racism and oppression within queer communities. You can *totally* be a minority and still oppress another minority.

Chicago is one of the most racially-segregated cities in the entire country. You have a clear divide between neighborhoods. You have a clear divide between North-Siders and South-Siders. You have the same thing in the queer community. You know that Lakeview has the most resources, so if you want hormones, you have to go to Lakeview. That's starting to change, but the TransLife Center, for example—a homeless shelter geared toward trans women of color that just opened up—is *still* in the North Side.

**Nia:** Can we talk about gentrification for a little bit?

**Van:** Oh my god, yes! That's a huge issue, too!

**Nia:** I'm really interested in the relationship between gays and gentrification. I feel like queers and artists are often the first wave of gentrification, then the people who *actually* have money come after. I don't know why that is, but I think it's fascinating and very troubling. Do you have any thoughts or theories on why gays are often at the forefront of gentrification? Is that a trend that you've noticed?

**Van:** It *is* a trend that I've noticed. My mom loves Bravo TV. I try not to hold it against her. She watches this show called *Million Dollar Listings*. It's mostly about this one gay white guy who's a millionaire and sells apartments in Manhattan. He makes millions of dollars in commissions off of what he does. But when he's finding places to live, he loves to look for "up-and-coming" neighborhoods, which to me means—

**Nia:** Brown?

**Van:** Right, exactly! "How can I move into this neighborhood and make it fashionable?" I can't really provide an explanation why, but it's definitely a trend that I see.

**Nia:** It's interesting that you say your mom likes Bravo, because it sounds like she's not a big fan of the gays. Is that fair to say?

**Van:** [*laughter*] Oh, my gosh. My mom is a complicated lady. I'm very happy and grateful for the support she provides me *now*, but it has definitely been an uphill battle. I came out as a lesbian when I was fourteen, fifteen years old. Things did not go well. It was not accepted. It was "How dare you do this to our family?! How will you ever find a man to marry you? How?" I had a bunch of family members tell me, "You just need to sleep with a man."

**Nia:** [*laughter*] Because *that* always fixes everything.

**Van:** Well, it does for me now! [*laughter*] But back then?! Back then, it was like, "How could you tell me this? Come on!" Ugh, I don't know. It's so complicated. There are so many overlapping things that kind of explain how I was brought up, and it really explained why my parents are the way they are. My parents wanted to be American—what is the term?

**Nia:** Assimilationist?

**Van:** There we go! Yes, my parents consider themselves *Americans*. They wanted to live in the suburbs. They lived in the city until I was seven years old, and my mom told me that they started to see the neighborhood go downhill. She said, "When the Italians moved, that's when I knew we had to move."

**Nia:** And your mom is Chilean?

**Van:** Yeah. Both my parents are Chilean, but they've both been citizens for quite a while. My mom is a weird mix between American culture and Chilean culture. She accepts gay people to an extent, but when it's her own family—I think a lot of people have this issue—when it's your own family, it's different.

I definitely see a hardcore conservative Chilean upbringing in her views on queer people in general. She's very accepting now and she calls me her son, but at home my pronouns have not changed in Spanish. I'm "la Van" not "el Van." I'm "he" and "him" in *English*, but definitely not in Spanish. A lot of my extended family still doesn't know, so I'm still "Vanessa" or "she," even though I have facial hair.

**Nia:** It sort of reminds me of this one time I was walking down the street and these little kids shouted after me, "Hey, hey, miss! Hey, miss, are you a boy or a girl?" It's kind of like, "Didn't *you* just kind of answer that question?" [*laughter*]

**Van:** Exactly, right? I love when that happens at the place I work now because I'll just have so much fun with it. At the beginning of my transition, I was terrified because I had no idea! I couldn't answer the kid! I was like, "I don't know if I'm a boy or a girl! I really don't! Can you help me?" [*laughter*] I used to paint my nails at work, and I stopped because I got so tired of my nail polish getting destroyed and of being harassed about it.

**Nia:** By customers or by co-workers?

**Van:** By customers. My co-workers will defend me to death, which I love them for. Customers were giving me shit about it, and I got misgendered more often when I painted my nails, so as part of self-care, I just had to stop.

I had this little boy come up to me, and if you could be "future queer," [*laughter*] this little boy was *it*. I was so excited, but also kind of like, "Sweetheart, I hope you have an easier time than some of us." He comes up to the register where I'm at and points at my hair and is like, "Mommy, that boy has pink hair and paints his nails!" I was just like, "Oh my god, you're adorable. Be mine!" But his mother was just awful. She was just like, "I know. Stop talking about it!" I was like, "Let the kid talk! He's just commenting." He wasn't saying anything bad. I didn't mind. This little boy, he goes over to his mom and whispers, "Can I paint my nails?"

**Nia:** Aww! [*laughter*]

**Van:** She took him and was just like, "No!" and then they just left the store. I was just like, "Ugh!" I think about that little kid a lot. I hope he's okay.

**Nia:** Yeah. Do you see your artwork as trying to create space for "future queers" or as being political in some other way?

**Van:** I was asked to create pieces to hang in a queer café. We were all doing a kind of gallery-style thing, which I had never done before. I was like, "People want to see my stuff?! I don't understand this!" When I was making pieces, I was just like, "What do I do? Besides my comics and some vague anime things, what do I draw?" I thought about it, and my favorite piece that came out of that had my comic self at the center and said "*I love my trans body.*" I didn't do it so much for myself, because at that point I had already kind of accepted myself, but for somebody else walking through that café going through the same thing that I went through at the beginning of my transition. It was for whoever needed to read that.

**Nia:** To know that it is possible to love one's trans body?

**Van:** Right. Yeah. There's a website called *We Happy Trans* that's all about focusing on the positive aspects of your transition, and I'm a big believer in that. I'm a big believer in challenging the traditional trans narrative: "In order to be trans, you have to hate yourself. You have to go through a period of either self-harm or harm from society, and you have to completely cut off any association with your former self." I put a lot of my "former self" as I call it—as I call her—into my comic. You will definitely see myself right now and myself five years ago interacting with each other in my comics.

I'm all about being more positive about being trans and spreading that out there, that you can totally love your trans body or you can overcome things, without having to focus on what we've been told.

**Nia:** Do you ever feel like there's a pressure to focus on the positive that makes it difficult to talk about the hard stuff?

**Van:** Yes. I've encountered that. I did experience a couple periods of homelessness. I do feel pressure not to talk about those periods because I feel like, "Man, I don't want to depress people." I really don't want people to feel sorry for me because that's totally not how I view it. I view it as something that I went through just like any other experience, and it's something that made me more resilient in the end. I never really knew, for a long period of time, where I was going to stay next or how I was going to pay for things or how I was going to fill out forms when I technically was not living anyplace.

**Nia:** You mentioned earlier that at one point you were working sixty hours a week while you were homeless?

**Van:** That has definitely happened. I was homeless and working at Walmart and Starbucks simultaneously.

**Nia:** And also in school?

**Van:** Was I in school? Well, half the time I was. I went back to community college to start a psychology degree. So, yes, at one point I had the two jobs, plus school, I was still running Soy Quien Soy, and I was still doing activist work. It was a crazy time. I kind of crashed and I started to have health problems. I had to quit Walmart and I pulled back with activist gigs that I was doing. That was last year. I finished up school and I just didn't go back. I think

Christmas Day was my one day off from everything, and I slept twelve hours straight. That was definitely hard.

**Nia:** Do you feel like, during that time when you were working so hard, that the activist work was something that nourished you, or did it just become something else that drained you?

**Van:** I think at the time I thought it was something that refreshed me. Walmart was soul-sucking.

**Nia:** [*laughter*] Surprise!

**Van:** Right? But it has been one of the highest-paying retail jobs that I've ever had. They started me at almost ten dollars an hour! That was pretty great. At Macy's it took me three years to get ten dollars an hour. That was great about Walmart, but the work was just soul-sucking.

At the time I saw activist work as fun work, but later on, when I started having health issues, it became just more work. I think I really learned in the past year to pace myself. There have been a lot of great events in the queer community here in Chicago this year that I just haven't been able to go to, and it's just something that I have to accept. It's a forty-five minute drive from my house to the city. The drive itself gets really tiring, especially with the traffic. Organizing just became more work. I try not to view it that way anymore.

**Nia:** Do you want to tell the story about how you had a brief stint in the nonprofit sector and then went rushing back to retail?

**Van:** I kind of feel like I have two lives. I have my retail life in the suburbs and I have my activist life in the city, so I'm always kind of going back and forth between the two. Sometimes when I'm telling my retail-life people what happens in the activist life in Chicago, they can't believe it. I think a lot of people—and I certainly did—have this idea that when you work at a nonprofit, everybody works together, it's all harmony, and everybody's there for the same purpose. It's totally not true! I'm sure it's more true at *some* organizations, but I was not that lucky...[*laughter*]

I met so many great people through my first nonprofit job, but it was horrible! I mean, who would run to Walmart? I did because it was just that awful! I never got paid on time. My time and my personal life were never respected. I never felt like I was listened to. I felt like trans issues really weren't seen as important.

Now I can recognize the signs of an organization that I really don't want to work with. I really pride myself on the fact that with Soy Quien Soy and my freelance public speaking, I'm working with people who have similar goals. We don't always have to be in agreement on everything, but I really like to work with people who I click with. I think a lot of baby activists have that problem where they think they want to work with everybody! Because *everyone's* great!

**Nia:** Do you want to warn baby activists what they should be looking out for? What are some of the red flags?

**Van:** A lot of people in the nonprofit world will be like, "Why are you working retail for hourly pay when you could be doing a salaried, full-time job?" They don't understand why I choose to work retail, but retail has some pretty sweet benefits. A lot of nonprofit jobs will pay pretty well, but they won't give you benefits! You don't get health insurance or paid time off. It's the flip side with retail. A lot of my co-workers don't understand why anybody would go into nonprofit work because there are no benefits. How can you live without benefits? But then the pay is shit. [*laughter*]

**Nia:** Yeah. I feel like being a nationally-recognized activist doesn't necessarily make you more "employable." Maybe this isn't your experience, but I've been self-publishing for years. I run a podcast. I do this web comic—I have a lot of skills—but I still can't find a job, or if I can, it's as somebody's assistant. [*laughter*]

**Van:** Right, right, right. I agree to an extent. When I started out as a little baby activist, I wanted to be everywhere, even if I had to pay to take the train or pay for the gas, because I was dedicated to the cause. Being in this for years now, I can tell you that unless you're willing to pay me to speak at your event, I probably won't be there. If you want my opinion written down, you need to pay me for that, because that's important. How can you be all for advocating for minorities when you don't support them financially?

**Nia:** Organizations that are all about empowering low-income communities and communities of color often don't pay their staff much and expect a lot for free.

**Van:** Oh, yeah, definitely. I had this event where I told the person, "I can't afford your entry fee for the event, but I would love to attend." They told me that if I volunteered for a couple of hours and paid half the entry fee, then I could come. I was like, "So, *I'm* paying *you* to work?"

I'm a cancer survivor as of this year. I had a major operation in January. For me to drive half an hour, take a forty-five minute train, do a twenty-minute transfer, walk four blocks, and then volunteer at your event, plus I would have had to work that day…?

**Nia:** Yeah, even without cancer, that would be a lot!

**Van:** Right? I'm still six months post-op. Today I spent all day sleeping. I have exactly enough energy to make it through my workweek, have a little fun, and that's it. It has been really hard for me as an activist to come to terms with that, to really know my limitations.

I'm so grateful for my Soy Quien Soy co-founder Ivonne. I want to be everywhere all the time. If an event is happening and I feel like I need to be there, Ivonne reminds me, "Ain't no one paying your ass to be there. They *want* you there so badly, then they can *pay* you to be there." She has really made me value myself. I really wish that everybody had someone as great as Ivonne to tell them that what they have to say is important. That it's not only important in a societal way but also important in a financial way. It sucks that we need to be paid to do this kind of work, because we really shouldn't. This should just be the nature of the world, but how else am I going to survive? Being a nationally-recognized activist, what does that do for me? I'm still working the retail counter at a bookstore. I'm still being yelled at by some dude trying to sell me a used copy of *Fifty Shades of Grey*.

There's a weird divide between what we value as real work and a lot of what we do. Like you said with your podcast—and me with my comics—"Nobody pays me for that." But then again, a lot of the things that I do are half for myself because I need to do it, and half for other people because I feel there's a need for it out there.

Transcribed by Weily Lang

## Micia Mosely, PhD

**Micia Mosely:** In 2007, I left my position as a school coach with the Bay Area Coalition for Equitable Schools. As a coach, I worked with teachers and principals to help make sure schools were serving traditionally undeserved students—Black or brown students, English learners, or special education students—folks in Oakland who had not been getting the services they needed. I really enjoyed that work but wanted to take a break to be able to focus on my acting and my career. I decided to move back to New York City and kind of reinvent myself as an artist. I had my first career in education and had been known as an educator in the Bay Area. People knew I did art, but it was more on the side. I left New York when I was eighteen, so I wanted to live in that city again and just focus on my art.

**Nia King:** Did you feel like there was a support network for that? I mean, was there a support network for artists in particular?

**Micia:** I found it. I wasn't sure. This was probably the first of what will likely be many leaps of faith on my part. I had money saved and no plan.

**Nia:** One out of two isn't bad! [*laughter*]

**Micia:** Exactly. I really wanted to stay open and see what was there. I didn't have a place to live, but I had friends, I had family, and I wanted to really explore from a place of creativity and not have everything be as regimented as school. I knew what to do with teaching. I knew what to do in terms of getting into grad school. Coaching actually opened up my mind because it's transformative work, and when you're in the midst of transformation you don't actually always know what the process is like or what's on the other side. You have a vision, but it's really messy. I was already used to that and I felt like taking that frame, applying it to my art, and going to a new-old city would serve me—and it did.

I was able to find WOW Café Theatre, which is the oldest women and trans collective theater in the country, and that was a home for me. When I first moved to San Francisco there was a theater called Luna Sea in the Mission, a women's theater that changed my life. I created a home and support and community for me here. Finding WOW in New York, I already had a framework for working with folks and trying to figure out that we're the same in this way but different in these ways. This is theater, and we're trying to do things. WOW and Luna Sea had different purposes, but they were both grounding for me. Having that frame from Luna Sea in SF and then finding WOW, it felt really familiar in a lot of different ways.

**Nia:** Was Luna Sea also trans-inclusive?

**Micia:** Not explicitly, and even WOW wasn't specifically trans-inclusive when I got there. Those are difficult conversations because many of us are coming on the heels of our foremothers who were doing this work around race within the women's movement. I'm thinking about the Combahee River Collective and *This Bridge Called My Back*—all the folks from the '70s and '80s who helped figure that out. I walked into WOW, which was a predominantly white space, and I was like, "Well, this is going to have to change!" [*laughter*] Like, "We're in New York!"

Even when I was at Luna Sea, I came during a time when there were co-directors—one of them was white and one was Black—and there was a play called *Skin: The Black and White of It*. That was one of the first productions I worked on dealing with issues of race head-on. So I had a framework for dealing with those issues.

I think for me it was interesting to try to increase the number of women of color who were active in WOW. I got there and was like, "Okay, let's change some things. I know you don't know me, but here's how I'd like to help." Then I had to deal with my own stuff around trans issues because it was very new to me. Trying to understand what it means to be what's known as a women's theater *and* be trans-inclusive if people coming to and participating in the theater don't always identify as women…it got really complicated. I know that it was a great opportunity to have politics and art come together—because people wrote plays and shows and had lots of meetings with lots of conversations—because that's what we do.

In terms of support, I feel like the support really happened through work, and I often feel that way. When you're working side by side with someone who shares your interests, even if they don't share your viewpoint, there's a bond that's created. There's a support system that's created because you're both trying to figure it out. I think once you get to that, even if you have differences of opinion, you're able to get some good work done and people can get open enough to be able to truly hear different perspectives.

**Nia:** Yeah. If you don't mind, I'd like to explore this issue of trans-inclusivity in queer spaces and women's spaces a little bit more.

**Micia:** Sure.

**Nia:** You explained a little bit already about how you sort of became trans-aware and how your politics shifted around that. What was the moment where you thought, "This is something that's being brought to my attention because it can no longer be ignored" or "Oh! I need to educate myself about this" or "I *want* to educate myself about this"?

**Micia:** It happened before I went back to New York. In the mid-2000s, I helped found an all-Black drag king troupe called Nappy Grooves. I always wanted to be a musician. I always wanted to sing, play drums, play guitar. I wanted to play all the instruments and sing all the songs, but I had no musical talent. None. Not my gift, and I'm okay with it, but it's what I wanted.

Drag let me do all the moves and act like I was singing and be all dramatic without having to harm people with hearing my voice. [*laughter*] It's a win-win for everybody! It also involved dressing up like a man, which was like, "Alright." For me it was fine, and when I started there were members of the group who were in their own process around transitioning and for me—

**Nia:** When you say "in their own process," do you mean they were going through the process of transitioning, or going through the process of realizing that transitioning was an option?

**Micia:** They were going through the process of transitioning in various ways. I say that because I don't know how they identify, if they would say they had transitioned or were transitioning. I know that people were exploring these issues in ways that I wasn't. I was just trying to be dramatic on the stage. [*laughter*] I recognized that it had become a thing in the group, not in terms of being a problem, but I became aware that we were relating to this performance differently. It was very personal for some of them.

That coincided with me going through my own process of exploring my femininity. I've always battled with being read as butch and the expectations that come with it. I joke about it, but I wanted to be the kind of woman that I am, which is one who wears a lot of pants. When I put on a skirt, please don't freak out. I'm not "in drag" because I'm wearing a skirt. That whole pushback has always frustrated me. If I wear a skirt or a dress, it's like front-page news, [*laughter*] and I'm like—

**Nia:** [*laughter*] Who's writing this paper?

**Micia:** Exactly! Everyone makes comments about my appearance when I present that way, and I don't know that people have always understood the impact it had on me. During this time, I was playing with femininity and what that meant, but then I was also doing these shows, dressing up in drag, and being in these spaces where we were definitely one of the only all-Black drag king troupes. We really focused on that—our songs were all by Black artists and some of them were explicitly political.

**Nia:** What kind of political songs were you doing? What were the issues you were talking about?

**Micia:** We had a lot of political songs by Black artists—four or five songs total—but one of them was "I'm an African" by Dead Prez. We all had shirts that we made ourselves with a big Africa on them. Mine was red with yellow on it. We had, in the choreography, infused Yoruban dances, so we paid tribute to Shango and Obatala and a bunch of the different folks.

So you can imagine us singing "I'm African, I'm African." These shows were mostly white, and so were the audiences and other troupes.

**Nia:** Were you mostly performing locally?

**Micia:** We did Black Pride in New York, which was the first time that my mother and godfather got to see me perform. We did another song by CeeLo Green called "Closet Freak"—not particularly Black, but very freakish [*laughter*]. It involved us stripping down to our underwear and swinging dildos in the air. I look back on it, and I'm like, "The part where you decided to invite your mother and godfather to *that* particular show…" That's when I began doing standup because I was like, "I need to start doing art where I feel more comfortable with my godfather being there."

My godfather and I have a forty-year age difference. He's my mother's best friend and helped raise me, so he's somewhere between an uncle and a grandfather. You don't need to be swinging dildos in front of someone like that. I love them because they are *beyond* supportive and were just like, "Alright, that's what you're doing now. Okay." It was more about the edge around sexuality for us, because everyone knew we were female, dressed in drag, doing these songs about being closet freaks, and doing these moves. Let's see, what other songs? Blackstreet's "No Diggity" and Shai's "If I Ever Fall In Love."

**Nia:** How long did you do this for?

**Micia:** At least a few years. It was interesting because I was the first one to leave the group. It felt like it was time for me, in part because I didn't actually feel comfortable anymore. I didn't like binding my breasts, it felt really oppressive.

We had a lot of conversations. Two of us were at Berkeley at the time—Matt and I cofounded the group and were both PhD students at Berkeley. Matt was getting his PhD in African American Studies, and I was getting my PhD in Social and Cultural Studies in Education. You got some theory-heads doing drag, so we couldn't just sing the songs—we talked *a lot* about it. In terms of that gender expression piece, I wasn't expressing anything that felt good to me anymore.

There was a time when I was more masculine-of-center than most, and there was a time when drag allowed that to come out for me and allowed me to play that out and sing when I felt like I couldn't. But again, as my desire to really express my femininity started to increase, the dissonance was too much for me. I felt bad because I felt like I wasn't able to really appreciate and be supportive of folks who were questioning and thinking about and dealing with trans issues because I felt stifled, like I couldn't be my feminine self in this role.

**Nia:** Part of the reason I'm doing this podcast is to look for mentors, people who can tell me how you make it as a queer artist of color, as a queer woman of color, not only trying to make art and make rent, but also dealing with issues of racism, sexism, homophobia, transphobia, and whatever else. I feel like in the past I've had a hard time connecting with older queer-identified or lesbian-identified women, particularly because I feel like it can be really hard to talk about trans stuff...

**Micia:** Mmhmm. Absolutely.

**Nia:** I have this friend who is an older Black lesbian also from Boston, where I grew up. I was super excited to connect with her because I thought, "We have so much in common," but then she was like, "Man, I don't know if I get this whole trans thing, this whole genderqueer thing." Basically being like, "Isn't 'dyke' good enough for you people? We fought so hard for 'dyke' and to be dykes." I think there's a feeling that my generation is somehow throwing it away.

**Micia:** I do think it's generational. I absolutely think it's generational. I came out my senior year of high school—April 21, 1991. I called my best friend because I liked this girl, and I had a boyfriend, who's now gay [*laughter*]. That's how it works. I had a wonderful, lovely, blessed coming out. She talked to me for over two hours on the phone. She said her phone bill was a lot. That was back when long-distance bills mattered.

**Nia:** This is a friend who is also queer?

**Micia:** No. This is Pat, my best friend since kindergarten. Pat is a child of Haitian immigrants and mostly hung out with her family. I was her one friend who wasn't part of her family. She has always been really supportive of me. She went to Brown a year before I left and had the orientation with queer stuff and referenced that in the conversation.

I think it's important to recognize the number of people of color who are college-educated and have access in the Millennial generation. I identify very strongly as a Gen X-er, roughly people who were born between 1965 and 1980, and then Millennials are the generation that came after, many folks who are coming of age now, between eighteen and twenty-nine years old. I feel like my generation kind of got a *little bit* aware. We were coming of age in the "gay nineties." I think the people who were older than us, the Baby Boomers, saw all of that, when "Don't Ask, Don't Tell" was instated and Melissa Etheridge came out. When k.d. lang was on the cover of *Vanity Fair* with Cindy Crawford, I was in college. I think that was really meaningful for my generation in terms of us feeling like we *could* be out.

The people who are in their late thirties and forties, we're a particular generation that came out of a particular time. For the folks who are older than us, all this was happening when they were in their thirties or older, so they have a different relationship to it. I see the nineties as a pivotal time in gay and lesbian history because of the access to mainstream media and being in the conversation. The reason "Don't Ask, Don't Tell" gets to exist is because *somebody was telling* and somebody else wanted to say, "I don't *all the way* hate you, I only hate you a little bit." It's a different conversation than "I just straight up hate you."

It's progress, but I feel like the main progress was in the conversation being in the mainstream media, the current issues being debated around marriage, around trans-inclusiveness—less so in the mainstream media. It's kind of this interesting battle of generations, because I do believe the battle for marriage is important, and I think it's a hot issue for particular people for different reasons. There are some people who are like, "This is a civil right; this is about being equal," whether it's their issue or not.

For other folks, it's really about acceptance and fitting in in traditional ways. I know many people who are completely against the institution of marriage but feel compelled to support it because it's an issue of equality. It's like, "I want *you* to get married, so I can not go to *your* wedding as well." Then there are people who come from like, "We don't want to be like them"—this us-versus-them thing.

**Nia:** You're talking about, like, "We don't want to be assimilationist"?

**Micia:** Yes. "We don't want to be assimilationist. We don't want to fall into or mimic straight relationships, so therefore we're not in favor of marriage." There are others who say, "I may feel that way personally, but my politics of equality outweigh my personal relationship with marriage." I feel like in that debate, many of the folks who want to fit in and be accepted in mainstream society maybe fall into the "civil rights" category, and they maybe still have a little bit of their own internalized homophobia. It's a complicated debate, right?

I think the older generation still hangs on a little to the "We're just like you," and my generation is like, "Mmm, we're not *just like* you, but y'all Milennials are *way* different!" I always say we're this bridge generation because I feel like Millennials are really pushing this frame in general.

This goes back to what I was saying about the number of people who have access to college and information because I think, of those of us who were college-educated, people chose to do different things with that education. We have zines, we have the Internet, which also jumped off during that same time period of the nineties. When I entered college, if you had a computer, that was a *big* deal. We had very long email addresses. By the time I graduated college, there was some sort of expectation of communication by email, and we know where we are now.

I think the transformation of knowledge and opinion has really jumped things off. We have access to more of all of that stuff, so I say that overall, generationally, Millennials are in a different place in the world. I feel like when we're talking about politics, identity politics, and different issues around sexuality and gender, it's going to go deeper and faster because now you can have conversations across time and space in a way that you couldn't have with previous generations.

**Nia:** Definitely. I feel like the generational resentment sometimes kind of goes both ways. I feel like from the older generation there's this idea that my generation doesn't realize how much the older generations have fought to get us here, that with our ability to be so radical and so out there, we're standing on the shoulders of those who came before us. My feeling sometimes is that the older generation just wants us to listen and not to talk. I think they feel like we've just thrown them away and that we're not interested in anything they have to say, or even acknowledge that they may have some wisdom to contribute. Is that something that you see?

**Micia:** I see that, yes, and I think it's more that the stakes are different. I feel like that happens with every generation. If you're between fourteen and thirty years old, there's a thing about being young where you get some information from generations before and you have the energy and the passion. You have your whole life ahead of you, and you're not really looking back on a whole lot. I think every generation has that, where youth are in this position where they're the hope for the future and the older generation is like, "If you'd just learn about the lessons of the past before charging into the future!" I think the stakes are higher now, in part because of the speed at which change is occurring, and some of it you can't take back. I think there's an intellectual experience that a lot of young people have, and I feel like technology has interrupted our ability to actually have substantive intergenerational conversations.

**Nia:** It's interesting, because the purpose of technology is to facilitate those kinds of things, at least in theory.

**Micia:** Exactly. When I say there are certain things that we can't take back, a lot of it has moved beyond a specific issue. You look at something like where you live—how many people live in the same place they grew up, relative to fifty years ago? How many people stay in a job more than ten years? There's a transience, an acceptance of another way of being, and I don't know if we can take that back. Maybe we can in a few generations, but right now there's a quest for freedom. There's a feeling of "I want to do whatever I want, whenever I want to do it, and I've organized my life to be able to do that."

**Nia:** Do you think we should take that back?

**Micia:** Some of it. I mean, part of me organizing my life the way it is…I need to talk to my godfather. He'll be eighty in June, and though he's been telling me the same stories since I was five, there's wisdom that I still haven't captured because I'm still not *really* listening. I just saw him the other day, and he's like going *in* about something political. I don't even know what he was talking about. I was talking about the Mets. He raised me on baseball, and I wanted to keep it light. He was like, "We don't have *time* to keep it light. We're in the middle of a revolution!" [*laughter*]

He marched with Dr. Martin Luther King. I'm not really engaged in it the same way. I know my work is political work, but I struggle, because he has *tangible evidence* of what he's done. I consider myself part of communities, but am I really part of movements? That's a very intellectual question. When he's standing there and there are dogs and hoses, he's not *intellectualizing* whether or not he is part of a movement. I sometimes lose a little bit of faith in terms of what's possible for us politically, because I feel like during my godfather's generation the steps were a bit clearer. You go, you march, you let your voice be heard.

I look at what was going on with Iraq in the early 2000s. You had millions of people around the world on the same day marching against the war, and Bush was like, "Alright," and carried on. That for me was a real blow. With the Arab Spring starting in 2010, everyone was really excited, and I was like, "Okay… *but* Syria's going through it right now!" But it's not in the news, so people are like, "On to the next one. What's up with Justin Timberlake's new album?" It's that kind of short attention span that the older generations don't trust, and it's not specific to queer issues. I think the generational divide is greater than it has ever been because of technology.

When you then overlay issues around identity—who we are, how we show up, and how someone identifies—it exacerbates that. I don't know if the older generations can, depending on who they are and the relationships they have, open up to the possibilities that the trans conversation has. I think for many older generations, their struggle was for acceptance for the ways they already identified and they feel like, "You have a new identity? We're still trying to get a pass for old stuff. You're trying to bring new stuff into the mix." That's a tension as well because if someone can come around and say, "I have a gay uncle, I can understand *that*," but then with trans identities it's like, "I don't understand, therefore you're going to mess it up for *all* of us." Those types of arguments are as old as any other in identity politics, and given that we're still fighting for the stuff they were...like I don't know what it's like to have a club raided or to have someone bust into my bedroom and arrest me.

**Nia:** Yeah, and thank god for that. Thank the queers who came before us...

**Micia:** Yeah, and that's their point. It's still not over. We act like because we have some treatment for HIV that the AIDS crisis is over.

**Nia:** And *who* even has access to that treatment?

**Micia:** Exactly. Now that we're clear that it's not just about gay men, that's also changed the conversation. As Black women, we're one of the largest growing populations of folks who are infected. What do you do with that? How do you come together? You've got marginalized communities fighting over resources. Some people are trying to bring folks together. Some people...

I feel like the way gay and lesbian issues got introduced in the Black community was through the "down-low" movement, as I like to call it. It was somebody's agenda. I don't know whose, but it set us back. The way we deal with intersectionality is complicated. Those who have access to words like "intersectionality," it's like… sure, we could go to a conference, have our friends, live our lives, but I understand that when I go to a family reunion it's like, "Oh, that cousin that I haven't met is *clearly* gay and oh, that's her husband. Okay. But why you trying to go to the club *with me* after the family's gone to sleep?"

It's because that person lives in a different part of the world and has set up a different life for herself and is more a part of that "traditional Black community" than I am. I'm more part of an interracial, multiracial community, and so the way sexuality plays out is different, because the Black communities I'm more deeply entrenched in are Black queer communities. What are we talking about with intersectionality then? I think it's larger generational issues. I do think some of that is typical, and some is very much about this moment in time.

**Nia:** So, you have two jobs: you work as an educational facilitator, and then you're also a stand-up comedian.

**Micia:** On my website, I talk about it as "education" and "performance," because even though I talk about stand-up, now it's comedic performance. Sometimes it's about burlesque, which came after drag for me, so there's always something I'm working on that is out of my comfort zone. Drag was the first of those things, but I enjoy performing in general. I've been up and down many different roads with it. When I went back to New York, I did more burlesque than I ever had before. I don't think I ever did burlesque until then. Now it's the hip-hop project. I think of it as performance because it gives me the freedom to do whatever I want to do, whether it's emceeing, video work, or what have you. My focus is putting a humorous spin on important issues.

**Nia:** How do you see your art and activism as being related?

**Micia:** I think that at the base level the content that I deal with, being who I am, makes what I'm talking about political. I think having an equality focus and social justice focus has more to do with what I'm doing with that content.

Gentrification is a big topic right now. You walk into comedy spaces and there are five comedians doing gentrification jokes.

**Nia:** I feel like that's very Bay Area.

**Micia:** Yeah, but it's in New York, too. It's about how it's treated, what you're talking about. One of the things I'm really interested in is whether or not my comedy is reproductive of things that are problematic. I think, "How do I get you open enough to hear what I have to say?" but also, "Is what I'm saying making fun of something that is inherently reproducing oppression, and not calling it out as problematic?" Do I assume that in your laughter you see the problem? Or are you laughing like, "Haha, yeah, that's the way it is. They're just…whatever."

I believe I get to count my work as social justice work when I'm offering a counter-narrative, because it's not enough to make a joke about X or to be a Black lesbian on stage with a microphone. There was a time when people convinced me that just doing that was okay. I'm constantly thinking about, "How do I keep the funny and keep the message, not only play to my audiences or audiences who I know would agree, but open up the possibility for others?" I think with the two fields I'm in, one is compulsory and one is kind of in the air, so I have access. People like to laugh and people have to go to school, so between the two I should be able to do some good work, but I have to check myself and make sure I'm not just a cog in the machine that looks different.

Transcribed by Sophia Lynn

## Yosimar Reyes

**Yosimar Reyes:** I grew up reading white people and like…they were cute. [*laughter*] Virginia Woolf and John Updike, Jane Austen. I thought it was cool—I'm like, "Damn, that's so cute, they be having these tragic love affairs." But then as I grew older, I found Cherríe Moraga and James Baldwin. When I found James Baldwin, it was over. I was like, "This is where I want to be." Everything that he wrote, you could adapt it today. It's kind of sad that the same critiques he had, you can definitely still do them today. That says a lot about the maturity of this country—James Baldwin told your asses a long time ago to get it together, and you haven't.

**Nia King:** You said that your first poem was a "small" poem. What does that mean, for a poem to be small?

**Yosimar:** It wasn't even a minute long. Usually with slam poetry, the average poem is around three minutes, from what I've heard. It was really small. But I don't slam no more. I think I stopped slamming when I was eighteen.

**Nia:** How old are you now?

**Yosimar:** I'm twenty-four. When I was young, there was this urgency to perform and tell your story and you had deep stuff to say. What I saw with the older crowds, the adults, was that it becomes very competitive. I'm like, "Y'all motherfuckers write poems. This ain't the Olympics, you know? Chill out." So, yeah, I stopped performing in poetry slams. [*laughter*]

**Nia:** How do you think your poetry has evolved since you stopped doing slam poetry?

**Yosimar:** I think it's evolved in the fact that I write for myself and I don't feel the pressure of "Oh, this poem needs to be this way because I want to get a ten" or "I have to perform it *this* way in order for me to fit the mold." I feel like when I've seen a lot of slam poets, there's kind of a way of performing that you're already going to expect when you hear a slam. You know, the fast breathing, the fast words. That's not how I like to perform. I like to chill out and tell you the story and converse with you, as opposed to, like, "Da-da-da-da-dah, da-da-da-dah" [*imitating fast speech*]. I *could* do that, it just doesn't feel natural to me.

**Nia:** You said that you started getting opportunities to perform through YouthSpeaks and that you've been able to build your career as a poet since then. It seems like you're performing a lot. How did that happen?

**Yosimar:** It's just been a huge blessing. I think for me it has come from the support of other people who see themselves reflected in the poems, or feel some sort of representation through the poems. I always say it's not about me, it's bigger. I've been performing a lot. I get invited to conferences and universities and different spaces, and it's sometimes because somebody sees my poetry and really likes it and is like, "We need you here. We need you to come have these conversations with us." It's a huge blessing because I don't think I'm hot shit. I think I'm your average twenty-four-year-old queer boy from the block.

**Nia:** You are kind of famous, though...

**Yosimar:** I wouldn't say "famous." I think people think I'm more hyped-up than I really am. I look at my life and I'm like, "Girl, if you come to my house and see the way that I live, you will see that I'm pretty ordinary, because my grandma still be screaming at me to clean my room and shit." [*laughter*]

**Nia:** Do you find it hard to get paid as an artist?

**Yosimar:** In the beginning I would be doing a lot of free stuff—like, you want me in your classroom? I'll come. I enjoy meeting people and I enjoy connecting with people. It's never about the money for me—it's more about the message and to meet people and make friends. I would choose that, but now I'm older and I've definitely been on the grind for a while now, so now I'm like, "I'm going to send you my contract."

For me, it's about respect of the work. You need to respect it, simply because it's art. It takes time to write these things, and I'm not a full-time artist. I have a part-time job, and it just so happens that they're flexible enough to let me perform and to create. Art is definitely something that we shouldn't take as disposable. It's in everything that we do. As artists who are community-based, you're not in it for the money, because you ain't going to get rich, but you definitely have bills to pay and people to support.

I'm still learning how to negotiate talking business with people, because I'm like, "Well, what's your budget? I can work with you," but I feel that making a contract gets rid of any other misunderstanding—like, "I'm not trying to take advantage of you. I want you to pay me so I can afford to come give workshops." It gets complicated when it's like, "Well, we're going to give you exposure." I'm like, "I don't need exposure! That's why I have YouTube and Facebook." [*laughter*]

**Nia:** When did you get to a point where you felt like, "I don't need to be working for free anymore"?

**Yosimar:** I think when I released my book. That was a couple years ago. When I self-published my chapbook and we made a video, "For Colored Boys Who Speak Softly." We put it on Vimeo and that shit spread all over Tumblr. I'd go to perform and people would want me to read "For Colored Boys Who Speak Softly" and I'm like, "I'm so over this poem. I don't even like it. This was such a long time ago." I was performing a lot.

I started taking classes with other artists. I was part of the Multicultural Arts Leadership Initiative in San Jose. They were very adamant about teaching me that it's not about the number of shows you do, that I need to take time as an artist to create pieces that are going to be profound enough that they are going to leave a legacy, as opposed to me busting my ass going from show to show to show and repeating the same poems, when I don't even have money to take a couple days off and write something that's profound enough for people to be moved. As artists, we're in the hustle all the time, but it's also important that we take time to create and that we're not overwhelmed by the urgency to develop more work.

**Nia:** I haven't seen the video for "Colored Boys" in a while, but I remember it being really well-produced. There are multiple locations, it's shot with a nice camera—clearly there was some effort put into the production of that video.

I guess that's another question: I'm super impatient, and it's hard for me to slow down and focus on making something really good because sometimes I just want to get it out there. Is that something that you struggle with?

**Yosimar:** I'm impatient, too. If I write a poem, I'll post it online. I don't even check if it's edited right, I'll just post it. If you understand it, you understand it. If you don't, you don't. But with certain pieces, I definitely like to take my time to honor the work, because I feel like if it's something that's really important to me, that I'm passionate about, I want it to be produced well.

Thankfully, I've been able to collaborate with a lot of people. I may not know how to do something, but they have the talent, like for creating a flyer or for making videos. That's how you bargain with your friends—like, "Okay, girl, you make this video for me, and I'll go give a presentation in your classroom or workshop or whatever." You help each other out like that.

For a lot of the videos, I've been helped out by my homegirl Jean Melesaine. She's the one who produces all my stuff. She understands me because we both grew up in San Jose. She knows a lot of my ideas and concepts, so we kind of balance each other in that way. Julio Salgado with the Dreamers Adrift project—we've done a couple of videos with them. It's also about connecting with people who have your similar vision.

**Nia:** How did you get your chapbook made? Because it's not like a zine—it's a legit book.

**Yosimar:** With that book, it goes back to collaborations. I was going to National Hispanic University in San Jose at the time, and they had just partnered up with this marketing company called Milagro Marketing. Their whole thing was marketing for Latinos and they were making flyers for National Hispanic University. I told my friend, "I want a book. I don't know how I would go about that." My friend was like, "You should give Milagro Marketing a call. I'm sure they haven't made a book, but they can probably figure it out." So I called them, met up with them like, "I want a book. This is the layout that I want. This is the kind of vision that I have for the book." They made it happen. They printed it out. It worked, it looked nice, and I was really proud of it.

**Nia:** That's awesome. I feel like this is becoming a little bit of a theme on the podcast now—people who are publishing with publishers that have never published anything else before. I think it's a really interesting phenomenon because publishing is this whole world—you have the publishers, the distributors, the bookstores, and the people who review the books—but a lot of the people I'm talking with are not connected to any of that. It's just like, "Oh, I had a friend. Then we put it together."

**Yosimar:** Yeah, that's what I found. I could publish with a publisher, but then I'm like, "It's *my* work." More traditional publishing would definitely help to promote work to a bigger audience because you have a team behind you, but at the same time, I was like, "Well, I'm nineteen and this is my first book. I'm trying to get my name out there so people see that I'm out here trying to hustle." I feel like it's like rappers putting out their mixtape—"You want to buy my mixtape? This is what I got." I'm thinking of publishing a second book.

**Nia:** How did you meet Julio Salgado?

**Yosimar:** I met Julio at a conference in Santa Ana. I got invited to speak at a queer immigration conference, and at the time Julio was starting off, doing his drawings. That's when I met him, and we just clicked. I think he's very chill—he has this really mellow personality. I liked his work. I'm like, "Well, I don't know how to draw, so I got you."

We definitely connected. We were so happy that we were both queer undocumented artists and we're both little gay boys. Then we started working together and collaborating. We kind of had similar experiences because we're both hustling right now, because we're both queer and undocumented. We're in high demand because immigration and queerness are really popular topics right now. Everybody wants to write a paper about you. Everybody wants you to come talk to their school about the intersections of immigration and sexuality, all that stuff. Julio and I are like, "We're like Kelly and Beyoncé right now." [*laughter*]

But I'm more than queer and undocumented. If you're going to invite me to your classroom to speak on it, I'm going to speak on it. It might not be your conventional narrative of what it means to be undocumented, because I'm not at that point where I'm dwelling on how bad it is. I'm trying to see the blessings and the good in it. It'll definitely be something different than me crying because I'm undocumented. It's hard! But I'm not going to cry. [*laughter*]

**Nia:** Do you think that's what people are looking for?

**Yosimar:** A lot of times, I feel like people are sadistic in that way. When they go to a poetry reading or a poetry slam, people like to hear about tragic shit. I feel like if that's your pain, and you want to share it, by all means, share it. Get it out. But for me, if I have ten poems and nine of them are about my traumas, then I have one that's just happy, about the sun. You know, some days I just want to write about the sun.

When I write, it's about what I'm feeling. If I'm heartbroken, I'm going to write something sad, but I'm always trying to see the whole picture. You know, "When one door closes, another one opens." Cheesy shit like that gets me through the day. [*laughter*] I definitely want to write a one-man show. I think a lot about doing more, like, comedy work. I feel like I'm pretty funny.

**Nia:** You are.

**Yosimar:** It took me forever to identify as a poet, so I'm not going to be calling myself a comedian anytime soon. I feel like there's a kind of respect you've got to give to the craft. You need to put in work before you be labeling yourself something that you haven't really studied or developed.

**Nia:** I'm curious about what it took for you to be able to call yourself a poet and what the barriers to that might have been.

**Yosimar:** I have an immigrant complex—I always feel like I'm not good enough. I think that's the conditioning that I grew up with. Even though hella people might be applauding or liking you or be messaging you about how profound your work is, you still be like, "I'm not good enough." Yesterday, I was reading the manuscript for my second book and I'm like, "Damn, this is pretty good. I can't believe I wrote this. This is good."

**Nia:** I've been thinking about the stereotype of the tortured artist a lot lately. I think the reason it exists is because creative people are so ambitious that they're never satisfied with their own work. I think that's why we push ourselves so hard, and often why we're so unhappy! [*laughter*]

**Yosimar:** I think it's because I've been through so much that right now I'm definitely more on the positive tip. I feel like that's going to help me make it through. Right now, with immigration and everything that's happening, anything could happen. I could be gone tomorrow. I'm trying to find peace within myself to know that if it ever came down to it and I had to bounce, I'm going to be happy wherever the hell I go. I'm not going to be stressing.

I think I had that realization when I was performing. I had just gotten this gig to perform at Pomona College, this huge gig. I was going to be performing at a women-of-color conference. The night before, Carlos Santana had come to see me perform at La Peña Cultural Center with Harry Belafonte.

**Nia:** Holy shit! [*laughter*]

**Yosimar:** *Isn't that some crazy shit?!* I had dinner with them after my performance and they were like, "We want you to perform at Harry Belafonte's event." I was like, "I'm already booked and I'm performing on the same day in Pomona. I'm flying out tomorrow morning." They're like, "We're going to fly you back the same night. Then we'll pick you up and we'll take you to the event." I'm like, "I'm down!" So there I am performing for all these women of color. Then I had to fly back to the Bay Area the same night. I'm like, "Damn, this is really happening. People are really picking up the work. It's so amazing, it's so cool."

I get to the TSA line at the airport. I was traveling with my Mexican ID because I don't have a California ID. I get stopped by Homeland Security. There's this butch lesbian. She was like, "Why do you have this ID? This ID tells me you're not supposed to be in this country." I'm like, what, nineteen, twenty, so I'm fairly young. I don't know a lot. This is the first time I'm traveling on a plane. Then she's like, "You're not supposed to have this ID."

Then the hood in me comes in and I'm like, *lies*—"I have dual citizenship and I called Southwest and they said I would not have no trouble traveling with this ID, so I do not understand why you are harassing me." [*laughter*] It's kind of sad—you've got to have middle-class entitlement, like "Why are you bothering me?" for people to respect you. I was thinking, "I'm going to run this all the way because I'm about to be in a detention center right now." She calls her little friend, another ICE agent.

These two people, they have no human expression. In my head, I was like, "What makes you human? Why do you do this job?" I understand you've got to pay your bills and I respect that, but just knowing that you have to detach yourself to protect a system that doesn't really care about you...They kept asking me questions, like what grade I got in recess. I'm thinking, "That's a dumb question—you don't get grades in recess."

Then they asked me, "What are monkey bars?" and I go, "What the hell?" [*laughter*] They were getting all mad because that was my reaction—like, "*What?! Monkey bars? Recess?*" They're like, "Why can't you answer the questions?" Screaming at me. I'm like, "They're out of context. If you give me some context for why I'm answering these questions, I will gladly answer them." I'm undocumented, not stupid. [*laughter*] In the end, she let me go.

I get on my plane. It was when we took off that I began just crying. The whole way I was just bawling because it was the scariest thing I've ever experienced. I kept thinking about my grandparents. All these emotions—like, why are they doing that? How can you violate someone like that and just go about your day?

Then I performed, and I'm like, "What a crazy juxtaposition. I'm here performing because Carlos Santana and Harry Belafonte asked me to come, but I just got harassed trying to get on a plane." That's what made me realize that no matter how good of a motherfucking poet I am, no matter if I'm putting hella work into the community, no matter if I am doing everything to be a good immigrant, to them I'm always going to be expendable. That's when I realized it's not going to be about them—it's going to be about me and whatever it is that I need to do. That's when I decided to start telling funny stories and doing funny shit, because I feel like I need to be sane.

**Nia:** When you got to the show, did you get a chance to process at all or talk about what happened to you?

**Yosimar:** I said it to the audience. I was like, "I'm so happy I'm here because I was about to be deported." It sucks. I've been having nightmares about it, but now because I talk about it and I write about it, I manage to laugh about how silly that shit was. I'm kind of over it. I still get anxiety when I'm traveling on a plane and I have to go show my ID, but now I know that, well, it's not going to be convenient for them to come after me because I know a lot of people. [*laughter*]

**Nia:** After your show at La Peña, Harry Belafonte and Carlos Santana just came up to you and were like, "Hey, have dinner with us"?

**Yosimar:** No, Carlos came to my show. I was going to National Hispanic University, and he came to give money or something to the school. The university asked me to come in to thank him. I'm always very particular about thanking rich people. They asked me to bring my grandma, and I was like, "I'm not going to bring her. I'm not going to exploit my grandma just because somebody gave me money." I went by myself and I didn't know it was Carlos Santana until I got in. Then I was like, "Shit, I should've brought her!"

**Nia:** Do you find that there are times where you're doing back-to-back shows and other times you might have a dry spell, or is the work pretty consistent?

**Yosimar:** It depends. Lately, it's been back-to-back. It's been three shows a week for the past four weeks.

**Nia:** Do you think that's because it's Pride season?

**Yosimar:** In June, I definitely get more booked. I do the university circuits and people are producing shows in the spring, so they're inviting me to perform and speak. It's crazy because I still have a part-time job. So it's managing that, and managing getting put into the shows, and traveling. But performing is something that I like, so I feel really, really blessed that I get to do it and that people invite me. I'm blessed in the fact that I haven't really had to send my work out for people to pick me up. People just find it online and they'll look you up on Facebook—"Send me your email. We want to bring you to our classroom!" I always feel really honored. Then these people become my friends.

**Nia:** I'm trying to promote myself as an artist on social media, but I also worry about stuff I say on Twitter or on Facebook at some point costing me a job. Some other artists I've talked to say, "I can't do interviews because every time I speak, I lose work."

**Yosimar:** I'm from Eastside San Jose, so the way that I speak or write or converse with people, it's not your most conventional, safe-space kind of language because we don't do that over there. I perform in a lot of academic settings, a lot of queer spaces, and we queers kind of develop all these theories and concepts of how to create comfort for one another because we've definitely been through a lot of things.

But I feel that a lot of times those methods are not really practical. You can't really implement them when you're working with kids who are not in an academic setting. I feel like it's important that we do that type of work, but also remember that there are kids who are never going to get into this school, and there are kids who are going to come to this conference and they're not even going to know what the fuck you're saying. You'll be here talking about "I" statements and safe space, and these kids are like, "What the hell is that?" It's very important to start developing language that's more accessible. I remember when I initially started coming and performing in academia, you go around introducing yourself and people are like, "Oh, state your preferred gender pronoun," and your ass be like, "What the fuck is a pronoun?"

A lot of times my friends felt really intimidated coming to my shows or to the conferences I would invite them to, because they're like, "Oh, no, Yosi, that's for your smart-people friends. It's not for me. I don't know what to say when I'm in those spaces." I always find it really heartbreaking that we're over here being revolutionaries and all about social justice, but there are people who don't have time to contemplate their oppression because they're too busy surviving. They don't really put labels on themselves. It's also about doing work in a grounded way so that it becomes transformative, as opposed to just being in a bubble of queers.

**Nia:** I think things like asking about pronouns do come from a place of trying to make a space safer or more accessible. I also totally hear what you're saying about how that in itself might feel inaccessible to other people.

**Yosimar:** Where I'm from, it's not like we're crazy—you learn concepts of respect, right? If I meet you and you tell me you have a problem with me referring to you a certain way, people make a note. I think it's common to know respect. People know it, unless you're a motherfucking asshole and you just want to be offending people. I feel that when you break it down, when it's simple and not so theory-based, people will get it.

**Nia:** I guess my question is how do you create a space where both the person who has pronouns that maybe you haven't heard before *and* the person who doesn't know what a pronoun is feel equally welcome at the table?

**Yosimar:** I definitely want to explore how to make language more accessible, how to make this concept of safe spaces something we can bring to violent spaces. How do you make a safe space when there are people getting shot just outside your front door? Instead of being in that academic bubble, we need to get out and go explore, talk to your neighbors, talk to your parents. I feel like that's what happens with a lot of intellectual queers—we like to theorize and shit, but we don't even know how to have conversations with our own families about the things that we feel. If you can't explain your theory to your grandma, then how useful it is, really?

**Nia:** That's something that I struggle with a lot. How do you translate your work for other generations?

**Yosimar:** Maybe they haven't really seen this before. I know we're not supposed to be educating people. I know that I'm not supposed to be constantly teaching you about what's right, what's wrong. For me it's more that if I want to be your friend, I've got to do whatever I need to do to convince you. It's like being a good Christian—I've got to be understanding.

Sometimes when I perform at college campuses, I'm like, "I'm going to perform for all these straight people and they're not going to get this poem. They're going to be like, 'Ew, that's gross.'" When I perform in high schools, that's when I'm the most shocked—"Oh my god, all these little hood-ass straight kids over here and I'm about to do my gay-ass poems." It's scary! Like, I don't want them to feel like I'm disrespecting them or anything. What I find pleasure in is when, after I do a poem, I have, like, the thuggest-ass cholito kid come up to me and be like, "Hey, yo, dude, I really like your poem. That shit was tight." I'm like, [*nervously*] "Oh, okay, thank you!" [*laughter*]

It's definitely hard when you're having those conversations about queerness with your family. Just because they raised you and you grew up with them doesn't mean they really know what's happening inside of you. But by having those conversations you're not just helping yourself, you're helping them and you're both growing, and you're both letting go of all these conceptions that you have of one another.

**Nia:** Is there anything that you want to plug or anything else you want to say about your work?

**Yosimar:** I'm finally finishing school. I'm going to be starting at San Francisco State University in the fall, which I'm excited about. I'm going to be a little nerd. I think I'm going to take more time to develop something that I'm going to be really proud to showcase. I think right now I'm going to take a break from being on the hustle all the time and focus on school. I really want to finish and be a little nerd with cute graduation pictures.

**Nia:** [*laughter*] Are you going for undergrad or grad school?

**Yosimar:** My undergrad. I'm going to be a junior. I'm transferring. The struggle I've had with academia is that I couldn't get to school because I've had to pay everything out of pocket. It's crazy, but I won't have debt when I graduate. I'm happy. I'm going to graduate and I'm going to be taking your jobs! [*laughter*]

Transcribed by Gunjan Chopra

## Kortney Ryan Ziegler

**Nia King:** I noticed the term "intellectual hazing" in your blog post "Tips for Queer and Trans Students to Complete the PhD" and I had never seen that term before—what *is* intellectual hazing?

**Kortney Ryan Ziegler:** It's when professors from a different generation who have struggled to get to where they are do the same thing to their mentees that was done to them. It's like that phrase we hear a lot—"hurt people hurt people." I think there are a lot of hurt professors in the academy. As researchers, we're supposed to have an objective subject position. We're not allowed to really talk about how we're hurting. We're never allowed to talk about how we feel. When we do, we have to put a label on it, right? "*Autoethnography*." It has to become some other type of research. It can't just be "I hurt today" or "My colleague said something that was really fucking racist and I want to express that." It has to be theorized, like—

**Nia:** "I theorize that you're fucking racist"?

**Kortney:** Exactly. You become dehumanized as an intellectual living and working in the academy. It's hard not to project that onto people you're working with and to kind of make them feel your pain, too. It can take the form of anything—being unnecessarily hard on someone's research project and trying to find everything wrong with it, or just beating someone's ideas down to the ground. It's thinking that you're the only one who struggles and that the book that you wrote 10, 15 years ago is the only thing that we can look toward, that everything that's been done since then is nothing.

This all produces a really messed up type of hazing, which can make people want to drop out, to leave the academy. A lot of students build up this idea that graduate school is *supposed* to be psychologically and emotionally damaging. It doesn't have to be that way. It's like we just accept that damage is part of it, and that allows people to continue to intellectually haze and harm their colleagues. I think we have to change the way we think about the academy.

**Nia:** How did you end up writing for *The Huffington Post*?

**Kortney:** I was working at the Transgender Law Center, planning their annual advocacy conference, and as part of my planning I was doing a lot of writing to promote their event. Our communications guy wasn't able to write an article about the conference and I was like, "I'll write it." He was like, "Do you want to submit it to *The Huffington Post*? You could do a guest post." I was like, "Really? Yeah, of course." Once I did that, the editor for the *Huffington Post Gay Voices* section liked my writing so much that they offered me the golden key [*laughter*]. It's been great for me because I get to cross-post my writing from my blog, *blac(k)ademic*, so I get a wider audience and can send people over to my blog.

**Nia:** I really appreciated your article "11 Trans Artists of Color You Should Know in 2013" on *Huffington Post Gay Voices*. I'm contacting some of those people now to invite them to speak on the podcast. How did you choose who to highlight?

**Kortney:** I was just seeing who was doing work. Some of them I am a personal fan of and felt like they deserved more visibility. Some of them I had just discovered and was like, "Wow, I am so fascinated by the work you do." I wrote the blog post and it became a front-page item on *Huffington Post Gay Voices*. I was like, "Of course. This is the year of trans people."

It was awesome because I got so many emails of thanks. I mean, from the artists, who were very grateful, but even more so from people who were like, "I never even knew these people were doing work. Thank you. I want to bring them to my school. I want to interview them." I'm like, "Great!" This is what we should be doing as artists of color—supporting each other, providing more opportunities so that you can live your life and make money.

You don't have to do things for free. I'm not saying that those people on the list are doing things for free at all, but I like to show public support and take advantage of my networks so that people like me can benefit as well.

*The Huffington Post* had featured an article during Trans Awareness Month [November] in 2012, "Transgender Artists You Should Know: A Roundup in Honor of the Day of Remembrance." So few of them were people of color that I got mad. I was like, "That's not fair!" It went everywhere, that article, so I was like, "I'm going to do my own."

**Nia:** Do you see your business as being separate from your art?

**Kortney:** In terms of doing business with the trans community, I am in the process of building the capacity for an organization called Who We Know. I really want to take trans people of color with significant business experience, significant life experience, or significant educational backgrounds, and turn them into entrepreneurs and into companies. Working with me, they would be partnered with the resources and networks of established nonprofits, and use the nonprofits' money to economically empower trans people of color. I think there's a way to really shift those financial resources and human capital in ways that benefit trans people of color.

**Nia:** It's interesting, the relationship between nonprofits and business, because nonprofit organizations can't legally operate as for-profit companies, but there are nonprofits that *incubate* small businesses.

**Kortney:** I wish there were more non-profits that did that! I think that's the kind of model that I'm basing Who We Know off of, because before I transitioned, I had spent so long doing so many incredible things. After I transitioned, I spent two-and-a-half-plus years with nothing. I was depressed. I lost so many things that I need. I lost my filmmaking equipment. I almost lost my home. All the skills and creativity—I almost lost those because I almost lost my mind.

I met other trans people of color who had amazing careers and then transitioned on the job and lost everything, but who still have this amazing wealth of experiences and knowledge that could benefit others who are in that position. Why not pair these people with all this money that nonprofits have? Or resources, not even just money, so that these people who have a history of doing amazing, brilliant things can do amazing, brilliant things and help to prevent other people from falling into the same trap of discrimination and unemployment.

One of the other projects that I'm doing right now is a hack-a-thon. It's going to be one of the first things that my organization Who We Know does. The organization is called Who We Know because people say, "Finding a job is about who you know." I think that for trans people there's this amazing community of so many movers and shakers and power-players—it's about who *we* know. We know a lot of amazing people! It's about being a community and really helping each other. I'm doing a hack-a-thon for transgender empowerment, bringing together designers, entrepreneurs, developers, tech people, social justice activists—all types of people. They'll spend two days creating web content and mobile apps that empower trans people.

**Nia:** That's a really awesome idea. Has anyone else tried anything like that?

**Kortney:** No, so we'll be the first ever! [*laughter*] I'm super excited because hack-a-thons are happening all over the country. At first, it was about tech-heads getting together to make cool apps, but now social justice people are really taking advantage of creating apps that empower people in multiple ways. Oakland has hack-a-thons—they have Code for Oakland, where people come together and use the data sets that the City of Oakland has and make apps that improve the bus system or let people know which local grocers are open. I was like, "Why can't we have that for trans people? Why can't there be an app that tells me what trans-friendly employers are in this state? There's data for it already. Why can't we just put that together?"

All the videos on YouTube of younger trans men being so open about their transitions really inspired me, too. I was like, "That kid over there, he's living his life without shame." I was like, "What if there was an app that was an aggregator of all these YouTube videos, so that you could classify by geography, situation, race, and people could access all of it together in one space, so that you don't have to go to YouTube and do searches?" I was thinking about all these ways that we could put data together to benefit our community. The hack-a-thon was an idea that I came up with because nobody else was doing it. I was like, "That would be so awesome. *I* would want to participate in it." It's going to happen—September 13$^{th}$ through 15$^{th}$ [2013] here in Oakland.

**Nia:** You mentioned a potential app that would essentially be an archive of transition videos that trans guys are sharing online?

**Kortney:** Yeah. I would call them "testimonials" or "diaries". There is a culture of that on YouTube. Starting in about 2005, trans people discovered or created this community where they document their transition. Even before my 2008 documentary *Still Black: A Portrait of Black Transmen* came out, there were people documenting their transition and talking about it, showing themselves giving themselves testosterone shots or post-surgery, sharing things that they couldn't share with their family or friends or lovers, sharing it to a camera for a video that some other guy's going to watch or some other young woman's going to watch. This amazing archive exists on YouTube. How can we make that archive more beneficial for all types of trans people? How can we make it more accessible for trans people? Using YouTube's API [application programming interface] to create an app or website—I think that's such a powerful idea.

Talking about my idea, working on it, and finding sponsors has been an incredible journey because people are so excited about it. They're like "Wow, this is going to be so cool! Of course it's a great idea!" There are so many trans people in the tech industry, and people in the tech industry who have social justice mindsets, who want to use their skills to make important apps.

**Nia:** Do you have any concern about something like an app that's an archive of transition videos falling into the wrong hands?

**Kortney:** Yeah. I think anything can fall into the wrong hands. I think that's a risk we take with creating anything. Someone can take advantage of it, but that shouldn't stop us from doing it, and we should push harder to get lots of stuff out there *because* we know that it's so easy for things to be misappropriated and taken advantage of. It's why trans people should be in charge of creating work that centers us and focuses on us, and why it's important that we have a say in how we are represented. It's inevitable that someone is going to use what we create with bad intentions because we live in a world full of discrimination and prejudice, but there's also a majority of people who are going to use what we create for positive advantages, and it's going to make a change.

Transcribed by Amirah Mizrahi

## Lovemme "Love" Corazón
*Trigger Warning: Discussion of child sexual abuse and suicide*

**Nia King:** You're nineteen, you just put out your first book, and you have a publisher. How did that happen?

**Love Corazón:** [*laughter*] Friendship, magic, and a lot of hope. My friend Biyuti, who runs Biyuti Publishing—we'd been talking through Tumblr, and we're both trans women of color. We were having a lot of conversations about writing and gender. I heard that Biyuti created this publishing house and I was really excited for them. I was working on my memoir, but I never really thought of publishing through them. I just thought that I would write my book and find a way to self-publish it.

Then I started asking Biyuti questions like, "What do you do when you publish a book?" and "Where do I have to go?" and they kind of handled all of it. I honestly think that if it wasn't for them, this book wouldn't have been made, because I get very overwhelmed very easily by bureaucratic situations and processes, and I hate automated phone thingies, [*laughter*] which probably happens a lot when you're trying to get all the legal stuff done. The publisher is my friend, so that helped a lot. It helped to know someone who owns and runs a publishing house.

**Nia:** When did you have time to write a memoir while in college, and what made you want to do it?

**Love:** I've been writing this memoir for years, quite literally. For this memoir, I pulled journal entries from as early as 2008—anything from before that my mom had found and thrown away, so I had to restart, and I cherished those little treasures. I saved them somehow throughout all my moving and my journeys. I withdrew from the University of California, Santa Cruz in April of 2012. For a month, I was kind of just floating around San Jose with a friend before I moved back to Mountain House, which is this really small town in central California. I was living there with my grandparents for a year and I just moved again this last week.

During that time of living with my grandparents, I didn't have to worry about rent or food or anything, so I just had a lot of time to decompress from my year and work through my trauma and work on this book. I was very fortunate. I couldn't have done that in college. I couldn't have done it while working or doing anything else. The emotional vulnerability of writing just takes a toll on you. It was very difficult.

**Nia:** Have you been promoting the book?

**Love:** I'm doing the push now. To be quite honest, it's kind of scary to have my story out there. It's the most raw, vulnerable thing I could ever imagine writing. Initially, I had planned to just write this book for my family and my close circle of friends and community, just so they understood where I was coming from. The work I want to do is communal care, talking to other survivors and building a network of survivor support where we understand each other and don't shame each other for our experiences and learn how to heal through loving each other. This book was to give to my family to tell them what has happened because they don't know the details, but now I don't mind sharing it, so I'm promoting it more outside of my immediate social spheres.

**Nia:** Your family is finding out about all this at the same time as the rest of the world?

**Love:** Yeah. It's nerve-wracking.

**Nia:** Have they read the book?

**Love:** Not yet. I'm waiting. I sent myself a few copies so I could edit it—what I mean by that is I'm going to put sticky notes on certain pages and be like, "This talks about sex…"

**Nia:** Like content warnings for your family?

**Love:** [*laughter*] Yeah, pretty much. I told my grandpa this past weekend that I had published it. I told him that I was doing the whole process of getting the paperback first and marking it, because there are certain parts where the content is very personal, and I think it's a little TMI [too much information] for family. That's why I'm kind of giving them a heads-up, like, "You might just want to skip this page or two." It's nerve-wracking. It's really, really terrifying.

**Nia:** It seems like an incredibly courageous thing to do, to publish a book about your personal experience with trauma. Where does that courage come from? Or is it something other than courage that compels you to tell this story?

**Love:** In the last year, there have been a lot of trans women of color who have been murdered and brutalized, and I know nothing about them besides what's reported on them. I wanted to write this book to give everyone a background on who I am, to let them know that being a trans woman of color is a dangerous thing to be in the United States. I thought, "If I was ever murdered or if anything ever happened to me, I would want someone to know my story." I wanted to preserve my story. It was kind of just that I'm scared, you know? I just want to be remembered, I guess. I don't want my experience to be a secret.

The book talks a lot about how my trauma has been forcibly silenced. I wasn't allowed to talk about it, and I had to just keep it in for so many years. This is my way of breaking that silence. It's my way of not being ashamed of what happened to me. I've been theorizing a lot and thinking about how my abusers got away with abusing me. I have to carry all of the weight of keeping it a secret and keeping their personas and egos safe and keeping *them* safe, while I'm dealing with all of these triggers and all of this mental illness. It just seems very unfair. This is kind of my way of saying, "Fuck you! I'm going to share what you did to me because that was not okay and I don't care if my family doesn't believe me."

Some back-story: When I was fifteen, I finally told my mother that I had been raped as a kid for six years, and part of my family didn't believe me, so they completely cut me out and wrote me off as a liar. I could not lie about being raped—I had no reason to. I have four abusers from my childhood, and I only talked about one of them, and seeing everyone's big reaction to me speaking up about that one abuser made me feel like I couldn't talk about the other three, and that's why I didn't. This book is me confronting *all* of the abuse in its entirety and just being like, "I'm not going to be silent about this anymore."

**Nia:** Earlier you talked about the idea of communal care. That's not a term I've heard before. What comes to mind for me in talking about survivors supporting survivors is, how do *you* not get triggered? How does it not set off a chain reaction? I'm thinking about my personal experience living with depression and living with a partner who was depressed. I feel like I would try to pull him out of his depression and he would pull me into his, or he would try to pull me out of mine and end up falling in instead. It was just a mess. [*laughter*] How do you support each other without sort of falling into a cycle of triggered-ness, for lack of a better term? What does that look like?

**Love:** There was an Oakland screening of a documentary called *Secret Survivors* in January or February of 2013. I went with two of my friends and one of them was also a child abuse survivor. On the way there we were talking—"If we're triggered at all, we're here for each other, and we can hold each others' hands." That's what I call communal care—it's making sure that you have a community to support you while you're dealing with depression or triggers and feelings as a survivor.

During the movie—which is about adult survivors of childhood sexual assault and was the first documentary I'd ever seen focusing specifically on that kind of assault—I broke. I just started pouring tears and kind of clammed up. I sort of shut down and was very closed into my body. My body language was showing how I was literally trying to hold myself together. My friend's hand was just kind of lying on the couch arm next to me. There was this moment where I grabbed their hand and just had that feeling of someone else's warmth and touch. That feeling of knowing that someone was supporting me through that moment was very transformative. I feel like the documentary and that screening opened up in me the ability to connect to someone on that level and to support each other.

How do we support each other without being triggered? I think it may be impossible not to be triggered. It's kind of hard not to be triggered by each other's stories because our bodies have experienced similar—if not the same—traumas. I've heard so many survivor stories from my friends and my loved ones, and each time it feels like as they're telling the story they're also being healed through it. They're finally not carrying this secret alone, and even if I'm triggered, there's this love for them for sharing this story that pulls me through that moment. We're able to just be there for each other. I think the more you talk about it, the more it a) becomes real and not a secret anymore, and b) you find family who hears you, who just knows you. That's a really precious thing.

When I first talked about my sexual assault, I did not have the words or language for it. After talking about it so many times, it's easier each time. Now I can tell you all about it—I wrote a book about it! [*laughter*] I'm comfortable sharing the story. The book makes it real, but it also puts it back in its place, as a past thing. For a long time, I felt dirty or filthy because I felt like I was just reliving it. Now it's like I've lived through it but I'm also moving forward, past it.

**Nia:** Do you feel like using so many different types of writing in your book was a political choice?

**Love:** Yes. Ryka Aoki actually influenced the way my book was written because I hadn't seen a multi-genre book before. I bought Ryka's book *Seasonal Velocities* while I was writing my memoir and reading it I was just like, "Yes, this is exactly how I want mine to be. Poetry and prose and essays." I do think using different types of writing is political because my book is a mess—it's not professional, it's not edited by anyone else besides me. It's very much my voice. I love that, because I *am* nineteen years old, and I am not in this place of complete balance and healing. I am not above my trauma. I am not past it.

My book is very much me being this raw, young person going through these really tough emotions. It's me being fifteen years old, obsessing over my first love and doing really weird shit that I would *not* do today! [*laughter*] The multi-genre nature of my book helps because there are some moments where I had to write it like an author, I had to write it like a story. There were other moments where I *felt* it—there are moments I've had with my partners that felt poetic, so I wrote about those moments in a poetic way. There are other parts where I'm writing theoretical stuff because it's me deconstructing my place and my social standing as a trans woman of color. The book needed all of these voices because that's how I live—I live as a political person, as an emotional person, as a storyteller. My memoir needs to reflect who I am and encompass all of those pieces.

**Nia:** What was the process of putting your book together like? It sounds like a bit of a collage, in a way.

**Love:** It very much was a collage. I went through all of my belongings. I went through boxes of old letters and cards from friends. I quoted letters that I had from people, that I wrote to other people, and that I never sent. I also have journals from 2008 until now. Tumblr is also kind of a journal for me, too, so there are some posts that were private that I used, and there are posts I used that were originally shared online. I spent a lot of time transcribing the journal entries. I left those alone in terms of editing because I didn't want to alter my fifteen-year-old self, you know? That's just who I was at the time. I think that gives the book that level of real teenage angst. [*laughter*]

It was a lot of fun. It was really cool to just map out my life, to draw family charts, because a lot of my life is confusing and moving in so many directions. I had to draw this timeline and write down each year that something happened to make sure that my book went in chronological order. Even after all this work, there are still some things that are out of chronological order, but my book is a pretty coherent piece, I believe.

**Nia:** You're producing art and knowledge, both through video and through writing. You're also studying Psychology and Community Studies, which you described as social justice praxis and feminist praxis. The way you described what you're studying, it sounds like those things are really separate—what you're doing and producing as an artist, and what you're studying. You haven't mentioned what field you intend to go into.

**Love:** Psychology. I want to focus on abuse survivors and trauma survivors—their brains and behaviors, specifically, as a therapist. I really want to focus on new coping mechanisms and healing methods for trauma and abuse. I want to focus on healing through communal care, which is having other people come into your life. I think that's really important because currently there's this huge movement for self-care. To me, that's very isolating. There are people who need support from others.

Especially as a survivor, I needed people to love me because the kind of love I grew up with was very abusive. Had I done self-care, I would have just kept abusing myself because that's the kind of love that I learned. It took communal care to teach me that love is tender and love feels good and that people who love you will cook you things and bring you gifts and watch your favorite movies with you and make you happy. [*laughter*] That's the kind of love that I now understand as being love, but growing up, to me love was supposed to be painful or a compromise.

The psychology I want to go into would look at abuse survivors, see how they're coping, and see how adding a community who can support them helps. My part in that is being their therapist, that person who is listening to them, who is not just giving advice but building a relationship with them. I'm not entirely sure it's going to be through an office where clients have to pay me, but I'll figure some way out.

**Nia:** I could talk about self-care with you for a long time. [*laughter*] When I came across the term, I was working with the Colorado Anti-Violence Program, which is an LGBTQ anti-violence organization working to support survivors of sexual assault, domestic abuse, and hate crimes.

I was with the organization when Angie Zapata was murdered. The family didn't want to deal with the press, understandably, so it was my co-worker's job to serve as a liaison between the family and the press. Our phone was just ringing off the hook. Even though I wasn't dealing with the family directly, just being in that space was really hard. I feel weird saying that because I'm not the person whose family member was murdered, you know? I wasn't even the one who was talking to them on the phone.

Self-care came up in that context of "We have to make sure we're taking care of ourselves as we're trying to take care of others and meeting these needs in our community that are so great and so intense and so triggering." I feel like self-care is one of those things that sounds really great on paper, but actually in some ways can be kind of oppressive. [*laughter*]

**Love:** Definitely.

**Nia:** I think being able to take time and energy for self-care is kind of a privilege. That doesn't mean that people shouldn't do it or that it's bad. It just means, yes, we would all love to be able to take care of ourselves, but that's not always possible or doesn't always look so healthy. People cope in different ways. Are you familiar with the term "harm reduction"?

**Love:** Yes.

**Nia:** The idea of, like, you can't fix this situation, but you can help the person get through it in a way that is going to be somewhat healthier for them. I think the first time I came across the idea of harm reduction was through an organization that was doing outreach to sex workers. The organization was like, "Okay, we're not going to get them off the street, that's not even our intention or necessarily what's best for them, but if the heel of their shoe is broken, we can get them another shoe."

**Love:** I like that. I think about harm reduction in terms of drug abuse—that's the context I've heard the term used in, like if people are going to be doing heroin injections making sure they have clean needles. I think harm reduction is important—I definitely think if we're reducing the risk of infections, that's a positive thing. But that's not really going to move them out of this addiction. They have to *want* to move out of addiction. I'm very careful about not forcing someone to do something they don't want to do because we're all at different places and we have different ways of coping.

Applying the idea of harm reduction to my experience doing sex work, I kind of got stuck in sex work. I'd been doing it for two years. I started when I was seventeen, and I got trapped in this notion that a sex worker was all I was, that all I'd ever be great at was sex work. That was kind of because I couldn't get a job, and when I did get a job, I had to conform to being a man, which required shaving my hair, and that was the most dysphoric thing I've ever had to do. Harm reduction in my sex work was having condoms and making sure I was safe and checking in with someone.

At the same time, no one was really pushing me to get out of sex work. They had all kind of just accepted it like, "Okay, you're going to be doing this profession and here are some ways to make sure that you're doing it safely." In the past few years, no one told me, "If you quit sex work, your community will take care of you." I kind of had to do this work of saying to myself, "Sex work is not healthy for you." As a survivor, having these clients say really awful things about my body…It got to a really intense point where I had to shave my body hair all the time and that made me feel gross because it was like not having control of my body and performing in this way that wasn't healthy for me.

I quit sex work. It was really difficult because I was unemployed. I had no access to income. I finally decided, "I'm going to fundraise. I just want people to cover my rent for the summer and I will go back to school and it'll be okay." Doing that was really radical and revolutionary for me because I was finally asking my community to take care of me—asking them to get me out of doing sex work—because I couldn't do it any more. The fact that people had just been kind of harm-reducing was still kind of enabling me to do it and not giving me a way out of it, so I had to get out of it myself.

I know it's a privilege to be able to ask my community for that support. I have enough of a basis in community organizing and know enough people that I was able to fundraise enough money to last through the summer. I think about how many other people don't get that opportunity, how many other people have probably asked for that and then not had their needs met, you know?

**Nia:** And what about self-care?

**Love:** Self-care. Oh my god, self-care…

**Nia:** [*laughter*]

**Love:** Self-care. The way I've heard the term used has been very oppressive, like, "You *need* to be out in your community, you *need* to be doing all your work, *and* you need to go home and take care of yourself"—like it's another item on a list of things to do—"You need to do yoga, you need to 'go healthy,' you need to drink water." It's just like, yeah, some of these things are great, but you're still judging or assessing me on my level of productivity, like, "You need to do self-care so you can go back into the community. You need to do self-care because you have work to do."

**Nia:** Right. "We need you, so don't burn out."

**Love:** Exactly. To me, communal care is having a friend cook you dinner, going home and having someone watch a movie with you. You're going to go home and talk to someone or just do something with someone so that you're intimately involved with each other's lives. To me, that's important because in a lot of the movement work that I've done and am doing it's kind of like, we meet in these spaces and we talk and we organize and we theorize and we go home and don't talk to each other—"If it's not work-related, don't call me." I very much got that feeling from doing social justice work for four or five years, like, "We're here to work for our cause, but we're not here to be intimately involved with each others' lives."

I watched this documentary called *Free Angela and All Political Prisoners* last week. I absolutely recommend it. I think one of my favorite things about seeing the film was that there was a Q&A session afterwards. Bettina Aptheker, Angela's childhood friend, teaches at UC Santa Cruz and we had the privilege of hearing her talk about Angela a little bit. She was talking about how when Angela was released from prison, she went to Bettina's house. Angela had both of Bettina's kids sitting on her lap at the dinner table, and Bettina said she had this really powerful moment of seeing Angela with her [Bettina's] son for the first time outside of prison. I view that moment as so precious because they're so intimately involved with each other's lives that they go into each other's homes, meet each other's kids, and it's just like, "You're coming home, this is your home."

In the movement work that I see being done today, we don't have that kind of unity, that kind of family feeling. I never went into any of my co-organizers' houses and met their families or kids or partners, unless they were organizing with us. If they weren't doing the work, then it was like they didn't exist, you know? Communal care is having those relationships. When Angela was in prison, everyone was rallying around her. Bettina had some of Angela's family staying with her, I believe. That's the kind of support and care that I think is necessary, whereas self-care to me is very individualistic because it relies on the individual doing the work to heal or take care of themselves. I think that can be important. It's not like, "Abolish self-care, don't ever do it," but I would never tell someone to go home and take care of themselves. I would first ask, "Is there anything I can do for you?" before I let them go on their way. Self-care can be very much like, "Go home and recharge your batteries because we need you to run at full speed tomorrow."

**Nia:** It sounds almost like the Republican brand of "personal responsibility" when you describe it like that. Like, "Just pull yourself up by your bootstraps!" Even though in theory, self-care is supposed to be the opposite of that. "Go home and relax so you can…[*laughter*] pull yourself up by your bootstraps!"

**Love:** Exactly. I think there's also kind of a set idea of what self-care is, and there's this idea that doing yoga or eating good, healthy food…I'm putting quotes around "good, healthy food"—like, what does that mean? My kind of self-care was eating junk food. My self-care was going to see my friends because being by myself was not the most pleasant thing all the time, and I very much relied on seeing other people. I used to call it "self-care," but this is what I'm now calling "communal care." It's asking people to check in with me.

If I'm feeling really bad, it's hard for me to reach out to others. I might send a message out on Facebook or Tumblr and ask people to say nice things to me or to be kind to me. I think as a survivor that's really important because I grew up with this really negative self-image, so when people compliment me it means having new voices to wash out the old ones. That's a form of healing through community, because no matter how many times I tell myself I love myself and that I'm the greatest person ever, I don't really feel like it's genuine. When it's coming from someone else and I can tell that they're being genuine about it, it really helps in defeating my negative self-image.

Therapy was…I hate therapy. [*laughter*] You go into an office, you talk for an hour, you leave, and then what? Most people don't have a relationship with their therapist, like you don't go out and meet them for drinks—I don't think you're allowed to, actually.

**Nia:** [*laughter*]

**Love:** Therapy is very helpful for some people, but for me, I want people who I can talk about really heavy stuff with and then watch an anime, to be able to reach out to them whenever I need them and they can help me back. Through my asking people for help, other people have come to see me as an example. I've had people tell me, "Thank you for reaching out to others because it's helped me to also reach out to others." It takes a lot of courage to just say, "I'm miserable and I need someone to take care of me or be nice." It definitely wasn't easy, and it does take a lot of practice to get there.

It's also really important to know what you need. I needed positive affirmations because I would get all these voices in my head telling me I'm this horrible, awful, terrible person and it was so easy for me to believe that and get into this cycle of just hating myself. In order to break that, I needed other people to send affirmations that I wasn't those things. When I was depressed and also trying to support others, I had to just ask them, "What do you need right now?" If I was able to give them what they needed, I would, and if I couldn't, I would tell them, "Maybe not tonight, but I can try and call you tomorrow."

It's tricky, but one of the things I love about being crazy is that other crazy people understand you. They will not be mad at you. They will not judge you or be upset. I have this one friend, Melanie, who is absolutely phenomenal with my crazy. She just knows how to handle it so well. I will be withdrawn as ever and she'll still text me like, "Are you okay? I haven't seen you and you haven't been on Facebook or Tumblr lately. What's going on?" There are other people who send me messages like, "Hey, just wanted to check in about how you're doing, but take your time responding. There's no rush. I understand you're going through a lot." Just hearing someone say, "I understand what you're going through, you don't need to respond right now, I will not be mad if you take a week to respond to this" was just like… *great*. [*laughter*] I'm lucky to have these people in my life.

**Nia:** That's really inspiring. [*laughter*] It's making me feel good about life right now.

**Love:** Good, good!

**Nia:** Is there anything else that you want to share or say about your book before we wrap?

**Love:** The most important thing for me was to create something that shows unapologetic vulnerability, that really goes there, and then goes beyond there. I gave everything in that book. There are things I am ashamed of, that I am embarrassed about, and I'm reading through it and I'm just like, "Oh my god, I can't believe people are going to read this about me!" [*laughter*] But it's okay. I think that being this honest, uncomfortably honest, will allow other people to feel okay doing that, too.

A lot of memoirs and a lot of queer books I read, they don't really go into these deep places, you know? They don't really go into the depths of what depression actually looks like. For me, it was all about going there because I needed to, going there because being a young trans brown girl was difficult. Not having access to books about people like me, not having these real, vulnerable stories of heartache and trauma was difficult. I wanted to write this book as a foundation so that whenever I do other writing, people will have something to start with and I don't have to explain myself anymore.

**Nia:** Earlier you talked about wanting to write this book in case you were murdered.

**Love:** I have attempted suicide before, so I am no stranger to death. There's this moment right before dying where I either accept death and I'm okay with it and I'm okay falling asleep and not waking up, or I completely hate the world for putting me in this position of hating myself so much that I would take my own life. Then that anger empowers me.

A lot of the times I've overdosed on medicines, my heart was pounding and my brain went into this weird fog. I knew if I were to die in that moment, no one would know what had happened to me. Writing this book was very much like, "If I were to die, I would be okay because these stories are out there and I will be remembered. There is a piece of me that will forever be alive." It's documentation of what I have gone through and survived.

**Nia:** Like an archive of your life?

**Love:** Yeah, exactly. The book is very deep and dark and depressing, but my life is very deep and dark and depressing, so I think my work needs to reflect that. I know a lot of people don't really like to talk about or focus on trauma or depressing issues.

I think that trauma is something that people try to acknowledge but also are quickly like, "Okay, how did you heal?"

**Nia:** "Tell us the happy parts."

**Love:** Like, "That's so sad, I'm so sorry. How are you feeling now? How'd you get through that?" I'm no longer being traumatized all the time, but I also haven't healed a ton. I've healed some, but not a ton. I very much needed this memoir to reflect on the turmoil because there have been a lot of subtle and not-so-subtle ways that people have told me not to tell the story, to just "suck it up" and move on. This is me telling my story and being very comfortable with not "sucking it up" and being like, "I am a depressed, suicidal person, and I'm not going to sugar-coat my own memoir to make you feel better about your feelings because you're uncomfortable!" Like, "Then don't read the damn book!"

I just want to make room. I want to make room for depression. I want to make room for sadness, because [*sigh*] there is not enough room. There are a lot of feelings that are invalidated, like anger, like bitterness, like trauma. I want other people to read this book. I want it to sit in their gut. I want it to feel heavy in their heart because if they don't feel that way, then they're not really feeling who I am, they're not carrying me in them. So, yeah [*laughter*], that's how I feel about that.

Transcribed by Leisha Hussein

**Fabian Romero**

**Fabian Romero:** I am choosing to live a very unsteady life as an artist, which feels hard for my mom, or that's the assumption my mom makes—that I'm choosing this life.

**Nia King:** Do you feel differently?

**Fabian:** I feel like I don't have a choice. I've worked at a co-op. I've worked at non-profits. I've worked retail and done labor work. I've been working since I was pretty young. I started working with my mom when I was nine. Having had that experience, I don't think my spirit can survive if I do anything other than create. Creating has just helped me so much to survive this world and all the hardships. I feel like if I don't create, I won't be myself. I will lose myself, and I really believe that. I think my mom's starting to get it, too.

**Nia:** You said that you're interested in learning film?

**Fabian:** My hope is that I'll learn to make films so that I can document some of my family's stories because a lot of them are oral, and I can't do my family justice through writing. Their dialect is hard to transcribe because it's very, very specific to this small pueblo in Mexico of three thousand people, which is where I'm from.

I also feel that there are so many hurtful representations out there, and I would love to at least have a chance to do something that isn't so hurtful, mainly about masculinity. Everywhere that I see masculinity, it's represented in such a harmful way, even in queer culture. In queer shows, masculine people are yelling at femmes and stuff. That really gets to me. I think that we can do a lot better, and I want to try.

**Nia:** It sounds like you want to do PR for masculinity, to fix its reputation.

**Fabian:** [*laughing*] I don't know about fixing its reputation. What I would love to do is give alternative representations, other than the typical hyper-masculine, non-emoting, dominating, really power-hungry type of masculinity that's out there. I think masculinity has a bad rep because the way it's taught is really harmful. I would love to have art and writing and all kinds of creative responses to that to challenge and even change it. My hope is that my art will change some part of the world, or all of the world, or something.

**Nia:** By creating these alternative models of masculinity that are not based in violence?

**Fabian:** Yes! The men in my family…my father is not the best example of a sensitive guy. My father really internalized a lot of the masculine stuff, but a lot of the men in my family don't fit that masculine model and I feel that they're not even given a chance to be a character in a novela or a movie or something, and the times when they are, they are made into a joke. I would love to have something that challenges these norms. At the core of my writing and creativity is this desire to challenge people's ideas. I come offering what knowledge and experiences I have to help people see things even a little differently.

**Nia:** You've managed to build quite a career for yourself as a writer while you're still in school. How have you done that?

**Fabian:** I took advice from a poet. I met this poet while he was on tour and I was totally blown away. I was like, "I want to do what you're doing." I straight up told him that. Afterwards, we talked. We talked for like six months and he mentored me a little bit. A tip that he offered me was to use this chance that I have in college to go to conferences, to develop workshops, to get my name out there, and so that's what I started doing. I started putting my name out there, going to different conferences. I was definitely way too shy to submit writing anywhere, so I just started my blog. Just through sharing my blog with friends and having people get excited seeing me at different shows and conferences, I started developing a pretty cool...I don't know what to call it. I guess it's a fan base? [*laughter*]

**Nia:** A following?

**Fabian:** I want to be like, "friend base," but whatever. People started seeking me out and wanting to know when I was going to write more. It was really cool, so I just started going with it. I am a very honest person and I write about the struggles that I go through.

I got really sick last year. I had to have surgery. I got my gallbladder out, which doesn't seem like it's a big deal because a lot of people get their gallbladder out, but I didn't realize how sick I had become. It was an emergency surgery. Afterwards, it became really hard for me to eat and I lost a lot of weight.

I think that being well-known comes from having privilege and time you can put into promoting your work. I feel that being thin also had something to do with people becoming interested in me because most people who are pretty well-known have some sort of cute privilege. I didn't get as much interest in my work when I was heavier. I identified as fat. For a lot of my life I've been fat. I didn't receive as much interest as I have lately. I was really reluctant to accept that I'm more well-known now because I really felt hurt that people were more interested in me now that I'm thin.

**Nia:** Before we started recording, we were talking about social capital, and you were talking about thin privilege like you were just now. One of the things I thought was really interesting was that when someone hears that you are queer and indigenous, they might think you are marginalized in all of these ways and not think of you as a person who has a lot of social capital, but that's not how you see it.

**Fabian:** I've definitely built social capital, and you know what's interesting? I think this is true about marginalized people—one of the ways we are marginalized and othered is that our story gets exploited. It's the sad stuff. People really like hearing about how sad it is to be marginalized. In the beginning of my writing, I definitely went there because it's very much a part of my story. I have survived a lot. I think that adds to social capital in a way—to be marginalized in a queer community—because people are like, "You have a really sad story."

It's really messed up and it scares some people out of wanting to be a part of queer community. I have a lot of friends in my life and people who I've loved dearly who just don't engage with a lot of queer community because they feel like they can't move away from having people just be interested in their hard life. Yeah, I've had a really hard life, but that's not what I focus on all of the time. Most of my writing is very much focused on survival and my resiliency and hope…a lot of hope.

I've built social capital from just getting my name out there. I also have thin privilege and light-skin privilege. I'm also masculine. People are more comfortable with me because I look like these ideas of success—that masculine people are leaders and thin people get their faces plastered everywhere, and light-skinned people get more visibility than darker folks. It's been something that I try to talk about because these are my privileges, these are the things I'm going to write about. A lot of the things on my blog are focused on addressing those—masculine privilege, fatphobia, anti-Black racism, and light-skin privilege.

**Nia:** We've been talking about social capital for a couple of minutes now, but would you mind giving a quick definition for folks who might not be familiar with the term?

**Fabian:** For me, social capital is having power or being really well-known so that people look up to you. You're given this power in a community to shift conversations, or it's like, "This person is going to that event? I want to go!" You're given this leverage that people who don't have social capital don't have. I've definitely felt that. I think that's why, as an introvert, it's really stressful. I'm like, "I don't want to go anywhere. I just want to stay in my house and watch TV!"

**Nia:** I think of social capital sometimes as "popular people privilege," but it's not just about being popular—it's about *why* you're popular, why people are drawn to you. That has to do with things like race and color and weight. I also wanted to ask you, because you write a lot about privilege on your blog, do you think there's a right or wrong way to talk about your own privilege in your work?

I'm curious about how you grapple with talking about your privilege in an ethical way—because listening to white people talk about white privilege is something I have so little interest in—so I feel like, "Why would anyone be interested in hearing me talk about mine?"

**Fabian:** I've learned through trying different things in my life. I've learned by watching, actually. You mentioned that it's really boring to listen to white people talk about privilege. Seeing how white people defend their privilege, which is pretty common—people learn to defend their privilege because we're never really given the tools to really talk about power and privilege in our lives. It's been through seeing people defend their privilege that I've learned the things that I don't want to do, that I don't want to mimic, and the things that are hurtful.

I try to think about the tropes—what are the ideas that are the most used to put down whatever marginalized group it is that you have privilege over? For me, as a light-skinned person, dark-skinned folks and Black folks are usually talked about in this really unintelligent way and I have to make sure that I'm not doing those things that are really hurtful at the same time that I'm talking about my privilege. I have to repeat to myself that I have privilege—I make it a priority to because I notice that when I don't remind myself that I have privilege is when I make the most hurtful mistakes.

I definitely try to stay connected with people who check me on this stuff. I have friends who experience all the types of marginalization that I don't and I love them, so I really think about what I can do to be there for them and that's usually where I come from—"I want to be in solidarity with this person in my life." That is a priority enough for me to go out there and keep on saying that to myself until I find the right way to be in solidarity.

It's different for all of us. I feel really secure in saying that I have a lot of thin privilege—that it is new to me and I'm figuring it out. I've had light-skinned privilege my entire life, and that has really benefited me. I've gained a lot of access to spaces some of my darker friends have not and I've heard some awful things. Thinking about tangible examples of oppression keeps me anchored in my desire to work in solidarity with people who I have privilege over.

In the workshop I teach, I tell people to talk about their privileges with the same passion as they do their oppressions because when you start to do that, that's intersectionality. We are intersectional people. We have many different layers inside of us and they interact with each other. That's how we participate in the world. My privileges and oppressions inform my decision-making and they inform how I treat people. They also inform how I defend my actions. It's when I'm aware of my privileges that I'm more willing to change things.

Just keep reminding yourself that you have privilege and figure out a way you can say it that feels right to you. For me, it feels gross when I'm saying it to, like, earn points with somebody, but it feels right when I'm saying it because I want to be in solidarity with people. I've had to figure that out.

**Nia:** Do you think there's a difference between being in solidarity and being an ally?

**Fabian:** Absolutely. I really wish the word "ally" wasn't used as an identity. I think that when it is used as an identity people get away with all kinds of shit. It's a lot like having cute privilege. When you're cute, people don't want to tell you that you're fucking up. [*laughter*]

In my experience, in moments where I have been hurt by allies, people were perplexed, like, "Wait, but I'm an ally, how could I have done what you're accusing me of?" Once you publicly identify yourself as an ally, you go back into the cycle of indifference, not noticing that there are differences in the world, distancing and pushing away information. These are concepts taught by Leticia Nieto, a professor at St. Martin's University in Lacey, Washington. I also use them when I teach people about skill sets for working in solidarity with people.

Then it goes into inclusion—inclusion is like this conditional welcoming. You welcome people in, but you don't necessarily want them to talk about how they are oppressed or how they're not treated well in the group. You just want them to be there to make you look good.

Then there's awareness, then true ally-ship—these last two take the most work because in the world we live in, we're so rewarded for being completely unaware, going through the day and not necessarily noticing that there are any differences. Colorblindness falls into that "inclusionary" skill set, where people really believe it's enough to just think that we're all one people and so differences don't matter. That's actually really, really hurtful. Awareness and ally-ship are going against everything that's so normalized—that's why they're so difficult.

**Nia**: So what you're talking about with these different skill sets is a progression? It's like step one, step two, step three, step four, with ally-ship being the last step, the place you arrive at in the end?

**Fabian**: I wouldn't necessarily call it "arriving" because my understanding and the way that I teach the skill sets is that we fall on different learned behaviors at different points throughout the day, depending on where we're at and what privilege comes up for us. On really great days, I'm aware and ready to act as an ally for any marginalized group that I have privilege over, and I'm prepared. On some days, maybe I'm just really fucking exhausted and I'm just not in my zone, so I'm really indifferent or pushing away information. I really try to stay away from those attitudes.

It's not like a beginning and an end—it's constant work. The way that I tell people about these skill sets, it's like the more that you do the work to stay aware, the more you notice what skill set you're in so that you can push yourself along or get support to push yourself along. Usually that means finding people who have the same privileges as you to really talk openly with and also to be accountable to somebody. If you have people to be accountable to, you're more likely to stick on that path, but it's definitely more of a spiral or something like that.

**Nia:** One of the things I hear you saying is that being an ally is an action, not an identity.

**Fabian:** Yeah, definitely.

**Nia:** Earlier we were talking about your shyness and you coming out of your shell. You said that you started doing workshops and presenting at conferences but you were too shy to submit writing. I thought that was really interesting because I'd much rather sit at my computer and click a "submit" button than stand in front of people and give a workshop.

**Fabian:** I've actually been perplexed by my own personality for my entire life. [*laughing*] I find that in workshops I'm giving, I can be myself fully. It's when I can't be myself fully, when I feel like, "Oh, shit, this author is looking for this" or "This book is looking for a very specific thing" that I think, "I don't know if I can really do that." I mostly shy away from any situation—be it social or writing situations—where I don't feel that I can write about something that is fully, truly, authentically myself.

I am often seen as shy or quiet or introverted. People sometimes think that I'm snobby or something. Sure, judgments like that happen, but around close friends or even one-on-one with somebody, it's pretty easy for me. With writing, if I know that an editor is going to go through my writing, that's what shies me away from submitting. I have to have a relationship with them. I have to be like, "My writing is really important to me. Can we work on the editing together?" If I don't feel like that's possible, then I tend not to submit things.

**Nia:** Do you have a lot of experience working with editors and figuring out who is going to be a good person to work with and who is not?

**Fabian:** Yeah, I tend to ask around. I'm like, "I'm thinking about submitting work to this zine. Do you know the people who run it?" Or even if nobody knows who runs it, I read the publisher's information. I look them up and see what information they have out there about themselves. Usually if they have any points about power and privilege I'm like, "Okay, I might be able to discuss why my writing and writing process is so important for me."

I would rather work with somebody who is willing to revise things *with* me. That's usually what I say—"I'm thinking about submitting my work to you, but I need to work on this level." I can't have an editor chop my shit and tell me that things aren't right—at least tell me why. That's really how I've found people to work with. Sometimes I'm writing something that doesn't make any sense or doesn't have a point and it's helpful to have somebody tell me that, but I don't want the authenticity of my writing to be diluted or my politics to be diluted.

**Nia:** Is that something that you've encountered?

**Fabian:** Yeah. Power and privilege aren't really talked about in mainstream situations or writing that gets wide circulation outside of queer spaces. In queer spaces and academic spaces, those conversations do flourish, but outside of those spaces—and even sometimes within those spaces—I've definitely felt and experienced people taking my work completely out of context and using something from it that fits their agenda.

Somebody's taken some writing off my blog. I wrote this thing about people in academia, telling people of color not to believe that they are stupid because they don't understand academia, because academia was never constructed for us. That piece got completely washed down and made to fit this blog article about democracy, and...I don't even know. I was surprised. I was like, "I can't believe someone would take my writing and dilute it to that degree."

**Nia:** Did they actually change your words or did they just put your piece somewhere it didn't belong?

**Fabian:** They put it at the end of this very long article to make a point.

**Nia:** They didn't contact you beforehand or anything?

**Fabian:** No.

**Nia:** How did you find out?

**Fabian:** I noticed that my blog was getting a lot of hits. On Tumblr, you can see the people who follow you. I was interested because I was like, "Why the heck would this person with this blog name...?"—I don't remember now, but it was something really offensive—"Why would this person follow me?" I looked at their information on their blog and I was like, "This person has nothing in common with me." Part of their "About Me" was like, "I don't hate gay people, I just hate gayness." Another part was like, "I am pro-life and here's why." I was just like, "Why would this person follow me?" I started looking at my Tumblr StatCounter, and I was like, "Huh, somebody's coming in from this other blog." Then I get a message on Facebook from somebody saying, "Hey, just so you know, I found your stuff on this blog." That's when I read it. I experienced a very demoralizing kind of effect from it. I felt really sad.

I see it happening, especially to women of color, where people are quoting them left and right—bell hooks, Audre Lorde, Alice Walker—quoting them left and right to promote anti-gay agendas. It happens to Martin Luther King, Jr.—white people will quote him to promote inequality and injustices. I've seen it in academic spaces where people will quote Audre Lorde—and this is coming from homophobic people of color—who are using these queer women of color's writing to support their homophobic ideas. I felt like that was happening to me and it hurt really bad.

I actually deactivated my blog recently because it was happening again. Some people who don't have my values around social justice decided to call me really awful, awful names. I think they just picked random slurs and threw them at me all at once. The slurs actually didn't get to me—I think what got to me was that these were people of color. I'm there for my people. My people are people of color. To not have that support back felt really, really painful. I decided I needed a break after having my stuff taken out of context so much. I just needed a break. My blog is going to be back up soon. I feel that I've gathered more skills and resiliency to deal with that stuff if it happens again. I have a feeling it will continue to happen.

**Nia:** I guess in some weird way it's a marker of success that people are trolling you. I mean, it's also hugely violating to have your words taken out of context and used to back up an argument that is antithetical to what you're trying to say, but…I don't know…the Internet is weird.

**Fabian:** The Internet *is* weird. I've seen the words of people of color used out of context in so many contexts, even outside of the

Internet. Oh, god, I can't tell you how many times people quote Martin Luther King, Jr. and Gandhi in *such* inappropriate ways at times that are *so* insensitive to promote really racist ideas to people of color—"You should respond to racism in a compassionate way, like Martin Luther King, Jr. and Gandhi!" I want to be like, "Actually, *you need to read more* Martin Luther King. You really do! You should read more about Gandhi because your idea will be washed out. You won't have an argument." I kind of just roll my eyes because it's so frequent.

**Nia:** You were saying earlier that you're writing a piece about anti-Black racism within communities of color?

**Fabian:** Yeah, within communities of color. It's a really big dynamic that I grew up with. It wasn't talked about, but it was promoted in really strong ways. It's like, we come to the US to make it and then Black people were made the example of what it's like not to make it. I feel like oftentimes that's how oppression works—you're given a lot of examples that feed you this message but you never talk about it, so you can never actually make sense of it. You just kind of act it out.

What's really sad about anti-Black sentiment within communities of color and immigrant communities is that rather than building bonds with each other, some of our practices become really divisive. I want to write about it and also about my journey learning about the different mixes that make up my people. A lot of people in Mexico are part Black and nobody talks about that. I've looked at photos of Black people from Oaxaca and they look a lot like my family, except that we're a lot lighter. If we could just talk about the history and how we came to be this way…I would love to have those conversations.

I have some books that I want to look into so I can have a more thorough article, but I think that for now I just want to write a quick "how to respond to being called anti-Black"—or being asked to look at anti-Black sentiment and oppression as a person of color because it is real. It's oftentimes dismissed. People talk about some bullshit thing called the Oppression Olympics. I think that we're not going to get anywhere if we stick to competing about who has it worse because all oppressions happen differently. I will never, ever know what it's like to be Black in the world. *Ever*. Non-Black people of color experience benefits from not being Black.

How does that manifest in our communities? What can we do when we are told that we are anti-Black and are acting out anti-Black racism? I want to have even just a rough checklist of stuff, like, "Here are some things you should think about." One of those things is that if anti-Blackness was never directly taught in our homes or never talked about, it's probably because it's the norm—things that aren't talked about are the norm. I want to write about ways to get away from attempting to defend our actions as non-Black people of color and learning from that.

Getting called out is another thing. I don't believe in calling out being the only way to communicate to each other that we're being problematic. I'm also going to write about that—about calling out being a skill—it being a strategy that is helpful with people who know the language, who have the same definitions that you do, and who have the same academic experience that you do. Learning about anti-oppression in academic terms requires privilege. My mom does not know the language, but she understands the experience far more than somebody who's gone to college and knows all about "intersectionality" and can name-drop different authors. My mom understands oppression in a way that someone like that will never understand, so I think that call-out culture is not always helpful within communities that encompass different levels of privileges.

**Nia:** Do you think there's a right or wrong way to call someone out, or is calling out even a tactic we should use at all?

**Fabian:** I think that it's been helpful in some situations, but I would argue that if calling someone out is the only strategy that somebody has, they should develop other ones and prioritize working on other ones. There are definitely some people who deal with oppression in a very passive way—I would encourage those people to consider what it would mean if they actually told somebody that they're being racist.

We all interact with oppression in different ways, depending on our understanding of it and our education and also our comfort level with being aggressive or passive. People who are really aggressive—if you're already aggressive and you're calling people out—I would say step back and think about other ways because you're probably intimidating, so those situations are more likely to close somebody off from learning than they are to make them get it.

It also depends on the intent. If we're trying to be vengeful, I think that calling out works. If we're trying to get somebody to learn something, calling out doesn't always work. I don't want to say "compassion" as in "excuse behavior," but I think that compassion could help people navigate those spaces by being like, "Wow, that person is really conditioned to believe that's okay, and it's not up to me to talk to them. It's up to somebody else who has their same privilege, or it might be something that I can talk to them about one-on-one" if it's somebody that you have a relationship with, or if it's somebody that you love, or if it's somebody that you've experienced as being responsive to those situations.

I've also been called out by people who have a lot more privilege than me. It was done in a really condescending and power-imbalanced way where people were talking down to me. That doesn't make me want talk to them about it—in fact, it makes me want to shut off and figure out why it is that I felt so uncomfortable. My argument is that calling out should be *a* strategy that is used depending on the situation, not *the* strategy that people go to. That's what I want people to move towards.

Transcribed by Liz Mayorga

## Magnoliah Black

**Magnoliah Black:** It has taken so long for me to accept the fact that I am an artist. I always considered an artist to be something that I *wanted* to be. One day I had a crystallizing moment: I'm in a room with a bunch of other people who I consider to be amazing artists, I'm fan-girling out, and they're treating me like I'm their peer. I'm like, "Oh my god, I'm getting away with something—they're treating me like I'm their peer!"

**Nia King:** [*laughter*]

**Magnoliah:** Then one of them says to me, "You're one of us." I'm like [*shrieking*], "I'm an artist! I'm a performing artist!"

It was a really beautiful, frightening moment for me. I'm a performance artist. I dance burlesque. I write. I need to write more—I miss writing. I started doing public speaking about body positivity, too. I'm a creative spirit.

**Nia:** Do you consider your artwork to be political?

**Magnoliah:** I didn't for the longest time, but I think Heather McAllister has a quote—which I'm *totally* going to get wrong right now—that any time a fat person is on stage and not the butt of a joke or being made fun of, it's political. It *is* political. The fact that I'm taking my clothes off in front of people when I'm not even supposed to…I'm supposed to be *ashamed* of my body. I'm supposed to cover it up. I'm not even supposed to be a *sexual* person. I'm *not* supposed to dance. I'm not supposed to be approachable or attractive, and I'm doing all this on stage and I'm putting my body out there. I don't wear a corset on stage either—you get the full belly. You get the belly, you get the roll, you get the shake, you get the cellulite, you get *everything*.

That aspect of my work is political because I am, as a larger person, supposed to try to compact myself and take up as little space as possible to be the least inconvenient to "normal-bodied" people. When I am on stage, I definitely don't do that. That has kind of *flowed* out to my normal life. When I'm on the bus and I'm in the bus seat, if you want to sit next to me, then good luck!

**Nia:** [*laughter*]

**Magnoliah:** Before, I was scrunching myself up really small even if nobody was sitting next to me—or in my office chair, I was trying to make myself as small as possible. Now I'm all relaxed. I don't care.

My artwork is political because I am a fat person on stage. I am a Black person on stage. I am a person of color in the burlesque community, where there really aren't that many people of color.

Also, taking that beauty standard of a certain look—which is tall, slender, most often blond, has a certain eye color, things like that—and being like, "No. I'm fat. I'm Black. And I'm beautiful. *Still.*" Sometimes I wear my afro on stage. Sometimes I buy a *bigger* afro and wear it on stage. I think it's political in that way, reclaiming my body space and my beauty.

**Nia:** Yeah. I'd be interested to hear your opinion on sort of the rise of plus-sized women in popular culture, in terms of people like Rebel Wilson, Adele, and Melissa McCarthy. How do you feel about all that?

**Magnoliah:** I think it's good that we are *demanding* that our body shapes be present on television and in popular media.

At the same time, I think they could be doing better, quite frankly. I think we're still at this spot where we're like, "Oh, she's a big girl!" [*sarcastically*] Clap, clap, clap, clap, clap. [*croons patronizingly*] "Oh, how *brave* of you!" That gets annoying. Real fast.

Because you get a lot of that, you get a lot of that. [*sighs*] That is what they see you as first. They're seeing *that,* and they're not necessarily seeing your art or what you're presenting. That's the one thing that's annoying, but I think the rise of plus-sized women in popular culture is good. I think there could be more. I think that it's healthy for us to see a diversity of body types in the media.

I know as a kid, I was struggling to meet the beauty standard because I thought that I'd need to meet that beauty standard in order to be an artist or in order for my image to be seen. I was very embarrassed about how I looked because I didn't see anyone who looked like me on TV or in magazines or in books. I wasn't present—not as a Black person, not as a queer person, not as a fat person. I seemed to just *not* exist.

**Nia:** I'm realizing that all the people I named as raising visibility for larger women in the media are white. Are there particular people in pop culture who inspire you in terms of like, "This is what representation of our community should look like"?

**Magnoliah:** I'm not really up on popular culture right now. In the past three years, I've kind of slipped away from it because I've become *so* insulated within our local culture. Moving to Oakland and doing live performance, *my* heroes are people who people across the country don't even know about, like Juicy D. Light and Alotta Boutté and Kentucky Fried Woman. *Those* are the people who've become my heroes. Dottie Lux and Lady Satan—*those* are my heroes now. I found myself no longer having to search through popular media in order to find my heroes. My heroes are up the street, which has been beautiful!

As far as popular media goes, I kind of got discouraged because most of the images of people who look like me have been presented as very one-dimensional. They are the mother, the caretaker. They are the churchgoing busy-body. They are the sidekick to the main person on the show. Even with a show like *Drop Dead Diva*, which I loved, watching it was like, "I love you! I hate that I'm not present in your world, but I love this show!"

I got so tired of being torn that I was kind of just like, "I'm done with you, popular media." I'm really behind on popular media because of choosing to avoid those things, because of the representations of Black women—like Tyler Perry. I hate Tyler Perry. So hard. I'm going on record as saying I hate Tyler Perry! That's why I haven't found any images that I really like. I had to search so hard and then when I found them they were one-dimensional.

Also, I'm surrounded by my heroes. I get to *talk* to my heroes. I get to touch my heroes and people who inspire me. I haven't had a need to look into popular culture right now, which makes me very privileged in a way that some people across the country aren't privileged.

I think it's very important that we—people of color, performers, people of size, marginalized people who are performers—keep doing our art and putting it out there so that we *can* reach people all across the country and the world, because we're not given any justice in pop media. We're never the main event. We're always the side dish, and there's too much of me to be a side dish. [*laughter*] Like, *literally* too much.

**Nia:** Where did you learn your craft? Did you study writing or dance in school?

**Magnoliah:** I was made fun of a lot as a kid. I had these buckteeth. They used to call me "Bucky Beaver." My mom would put these curlers in my hair. When she took them out, I had this one roll of curls that looked like mushrooms. I looked like a mushroom. I'm really glad they didn't call me "Tip" because now that I look at it, I did look like a tip. [*laughter*]

I was made fun of as a kid and I went to this school that was mostly white, Roman Catholic. Most of the people there had some money. We didn't have any money at all. I spent a lot of time by myself, not wanting to talk because whenever I opened my mouth, people would make fun of my teeth or I would say something that the other kids couldn't understand.

Later, when I graduated, one of my teachers told me why my classmates couldn't understand me: "You were on a reading level and a comprehension level that was higher than them. *We* could understand what you were saying, but *they* couldn't understand what you were saying. I want you to know that."

Then a lot of things made sense to me. I often didn't want to open my mouth, so I observed people and I read a lot of books. A lot of my education, I felt, came from my own reading, instead of from textbooks.

I started writing through observing people. The writing kind of started in this weird way—fantasies, trying to escape from my life, which I felt was, at that point, oh-so-emo and depressing. I would get so sad: I would run into my room and throw myself on the bed crying and my mother, being the woman that she is, would throw herself on top of me, fake crying.

**Nia:** [*laughter*]

**Magnoliah:** "Life's so hard!"

"Yes, it is! It's terrible, it's *terrible!*"

You know, I had to stop crying because this grown woman is crying on top of me, and she did that on purpose! I'm trying to throw myself a personal pity party. My mom's with me and I can't throw myself a pity party. So yay, Mom, for doing that!

**Nia:** Is that where you get your performative nature?

**Magnoliah:** Yeah. It's *totally* from her. She says I'm nothing like her, but I'm *exactly* like her.

I started writing as a way to escape from that. I started writing as a way to *resolve* situations. Like if someone said something to me and I couldn't say anything back, *trust*: I had a story written where I said *all* the perfect things in response to them.

**Nia:** Totally.

**Magnoliah:** It was definitely therapeutic, and it got me through. Also, I didn't see myself in the books that I was reading because I liked to read a lot of science fiction and fantasy when I was a kid. Again, I wasn't present so I would write stories where there were people who looked like me. I didn't even realize until I grew up that, oh, wow, I was writing a lot of people of color in my stories. I made sure that all the main characters were people of color.

Later, I started writing more about my own life experiences as a kind of catharsis because I couldn't afford therapy. So LiveJournal became my therapist. [*laughter*] That's what writing was for me. That's how I got into writing.

I also play the piano. My mom wanted me to be a debutante. I had a cotillion dress and everything—etiquette training and all that. She wanted me to be a *lady*...and now I'm a stripper...[*laughter*] Poor Mom! Good try!

I played piano. I sang. I had a very musical household. My mom has a very beautiful voice. I grew up with music. Also, being in the city of New Orleans, there's music all the time, everywhere. I love jazz, blues, and classical.

As far as dance, I did ballet...until I got too fat to do ballet. I stopped dancing because I didn't think I could dance or act on stage because of my weight. I kind of gave up on being in the public eye, and eventually I stopped doing piano. I went through a very barren period creatively for ten years.

Then I moved out to the Bay Area and I went through my Saturn return, which was *brutal*. I'm just getting out of it. I'm turning thirty-two this year, and I'm like, "Yes! Saturn return is *over*! I'm so *done* with you!" It's not done with me yet—it's going to wait up until the *day* to be done with me. It's still trying to kick my ass a little bit. It's been fun. By "fun," I mean "dreadful."

**Nia:** [*laughter*]

**Magnoliah:** Right at the beginning of my Saturn return, I ran into Juicy D. Light and she said, "Come dance with us!" I was like, "Sure!" The first burlesque show I'd been to was the one I was *in*. My life just changed. I was able to be on stage and be present and be in this body again. I was able to *dance* and able to *move*, to *sing*, to have a *voice*, and to be a human being.

**Nia:** Was that a process to get back in touch with your body and with being a performer? You kind of make it sound like it happened overnight.

**Magnoliah:** Oh, it totally didn't happen overnight! It started in a dungeon because I'm kinky.

After I had been in this ten-year relationship that was *not* healthy and I left that relationship, one of my friends said, "You need to come out with me! I'm going to a dungeon, and you should come with me."

We went to this Halloween party. People were all dressed up, and it was great! I met this guy there—he tied me to a Saint Andrew's Cross and he took my shirt off, which we negotiated, but it was the first time that I'd had my shirt off in public *ever* and my back was exposed, which was at that point the *worst* part of myself, I thought. At that point, all I considered to be beautiful about myself were my eyes. That was *it*.

So there I am, back exposed, and he's flogging me and flogging me, doing it in this very *loving* way, and every time he flogs me, I feel myself dropping into my body, becoming *very* aware of my body. It's kind of like I had existed to the *outside* of my body—I didn't look in mirrors or anything like that. I didn't want anything to *do* with my body, but every time he flogged me I was *forced* to be *present*, integrated back *into* my body! Of course I orgasmed and it was *great*. Kink for the win!

**Nia:** [*laughter*]

**Magnoliah:** Through kink and through this loving relationship I had with my Dom, I kind of started to reintegrate myself into my body. My Dom was a complete Daddy. He was very much, "Did you sleep seven hours last night? Are you eating properly? Here's a gift certificate to Whole Foods."

**Nia:** [*laughter*]

**Magnoliah:** "Go to bed!" He was really serious about me taking care of myself and making sure that I had people who were positive and loving in my life. That meant a lot, having grown up without a father. My mother was my mother and father both, and I appreciate and love and respect that. She was everything to me, but I never had that masculine *whatever*. I didn't even realize that I had missed out on anything until I ended up with this Daddy-type presence in my life, who was like, "I'm proud of you. I'm proud of you." And…"Go to bed." [*laughter*]

From that relationship, I really got integrated into my body. I physically had to be put into my body. He supported me when I started doing burlesque. He was very excited for me. He took me out to get my makeup because I didn't know how to put on makeup, either. He took me out to get makeup, had someone show me how to put on makeup, and he came to the first couple of shows. He was very, very, very, very proactive in me doing this.

That first time I was on stage, I really thought people were going to hiss and boo. I did a duet with Kitty von Quim, who's my burlesque sister—love her—and I was expecting the *worst*. I'm standing there behind the curtain before I go out, and I throw up in my own mouth a little bit. I'm starting to think, "There are a lot of people. What is that *weird taste?* I just threw up in my mouth!"

"RUBENESQUE BURLESQUE!"

And then I'm out on stage, trying to swallow. It was real awkward.

But I get out there, I do it, and…they don't hate me. They're not booing and hissing and screaming, "Go away, fatty!" They're… *loving* it. They're *clapping,* and they're *smiling* and they're not laughing *at* me. They're enjoying it. They were loving and embracing and accepting, and *through* their love and acceptance, I was again reintegrated into my body.

When I got off stage, there was this belly dancer who came on next and I was able to watch her performance without comparing her body to mine. It was the first time that that *tape* was turned off—that tape that plays every time I see a woman walking down the street and I compulsively compare myself to her. This person was *gorgeous* and I was *happy for her* being so gorgeous because I was secure in my own self, in my own body, in my own beauty.

I did have—and still continue to have—ups and downs and ups and downs and ups and downs, and it took a long time for that *moment* of self-love to become the space my brain normally inhabits. Kink for a year, physical reintegration, and then that mental reintegration from performance helped me get to where I am today.

**Nia:** Is Rubenesque Burlesque explicitly queer?

**Magnoliah:** We're all queer or queer-friendly.

**Nia:** And your audiences? Mostly queer or mostly straight?

**Magnoliah:** It's a mix. I think performing for an audience in San Francisco, we have a lot of queer people in our audience, depending on what show we're at. We do perform for some mainstream audiences, so we end up with some straight audiences as well.

I think the difference is, with the queer audience, when we come out they're like, "FUCK YEAH! Fat women on *stage.* Give us MORE!" The straight audience is like [*stiffly*], "I'm not...this is *happening* and okay, I'm going to—" and then by the end they're like, "*Yeah!*"

We do notice there's an acceptance level difference when we first show up, between a straight audience and a queer audience, but we perform for both. We perform for body-positive spaces and for mainstream stages as well, and I think it's important that we do both. Juicy D. Light, our Head Bitch in Charge and Artistic Director at Rubenesque Burlesque, is really good about that. She's like, "We *need* to be seen, and we *need* to be out there. We need to become people's norm. They need to know that we're here. We can't just continue to stay in safe spaces."

For the longest time, we just performed in spaces that would be considered unsafe for us, somewhere there wasn't a plethora of fat performers or racial diversity. Recently, we've performed for spaces where we were more of the norm. I think both are very, very valuable.

**Nia:** Yeah. Race-wise, what is the makeup of the troupe and also of the audiences you perform for?

**Magnoliah:** We mostly perform in the Bay Area, which is very, very mixed. Race-wise, we are mixed as well. I don't want to sound like *Pokémon*, like "Gotta catch 'em all!" but we're very open to anybody who wants to come in and perform with us and put themselves out there.

**Nia:** Where do you feel like you are on your trajectory as an artist?

**Magnoliah:** The perpetual beginning. I say that because every time you get an answer to something or you think you've taken a step, you get a hundred more questions. It's like you think, "Oh, I'll walk to the store and then I'll have arrived." Yes, you've arrived at *this* spot, but now that you've arrived, there are just *so* many other places you can go!

I feel like I'm definitely going to be at the beginning constantly, almost like there's childlike wonder, where everything's an adventure and everything's a new start, where I can recreate myself with each performance that I do, with each number that I do.

I think I'm not a newbie anymore, but I'm definitely not wizened in any way. There's still a lot for me to learn, and I think I'll continue learning it for the rest of my life. At least, that's my goal.

**Nia:** Do you think you'll ever feel wizened, or will you always have that childlike wonder?

**Magnoliah:** Oh, god, I hope I never feel wizened! I hope I always have a sense of childlike wonder. I want to be confident. I'm at that stage where I'm confident in my performance but definitely still exploring, definitely still working on ways I can get better, ways I can reach the audience more. When people are really good photographers, you're seeing what they see, and when I perform I want to get to the level where people are feeling what I'm feeling.

**Nia:** How do you measure your success as an artist?

**Magnoliah:** I used to think that if I was able to afford to live off of being a writer or performer, then that would be success. I was so hooked on that idea that I stopped enjoying what I was doing. I wasn't being creative anymore with my art, I was just obsessing about it—obsessing about what other people thought about it—which tainted what I was putting out.

You have to have some kind of discussion or dialogue with your audience. It is key and essential that your audience is getting what you're trying to tell them and that you're putting out something that they want to see, but it also has to be something for *me*. I was removing myself too far from it, so I had to re-evaluate what my idea of success was. Part of success, for me, is my happiness. If I'm putting something out on the stage that's making me happy, even if it's completely tragic, then I've done good. If I'm putting something out there and someone comes to me and says, "Thank you," even if it's just one person, then I've been successful. If someone has felt what I'm feeling, if someone feels relieved or touched or inspired, then I am successful. My success is no longer based on whether or not I'm able to survive off of my art, but rather on whether or not my art has extended beyond myself, whether it has had a positive effect on the world around me. That's my measure of success now.

**Nia:** Do you feel supported here in the Bay as an artist doing the type of work that you do?

**Magnoliah:** Yes! I think there are definitely places where I have to hustle more or hustle harder, but there are stages for me to perform on. There are peer groups for me to speak to. There are trade and barter systems that we all use. We have a performance community here. We're very hooked into each other.

You want to hook into positive people because in every circle there's negativity and positivity, but I feel supported. I think that there are a lot of people who appreciate live theater in the Bay Area, a lot of people who appreciate freedom of thought or creativity here. I feel like I'm in the right place to do this. I do feel like I'm appreciated, and I do feel like I'm supported, not just supported for my art based on where it is now, but also for where it can go. There are other artists who are invested in making sure that I grow as an artist because we all lift each other up. There are artists who I want to see grow, who I want to lift up as well. I feel like it's a community and a family, and I'm very, very happy and proud to be a part of it.

Transcribed by Weily Lang

## Kiam Marcelo Junio

**Kiam Marcelo Junio:** When I was in high school, I was really intent on being this famous pop star. I had been writing my own songs, making beats on the computer, and performing everywhere. I've been singing since I was five or six. My first public performance was in my kindergarten graduation—I did a solo song. I've been singing since then, performing in front of people. In high school, I told my mom that I wanted to be this famous pop star and she said, "No, Filipinos are never in the spotlight. You will always be in the background—backstage—because that's just not how we are in this country."

**Nia King:** This country, at that time, being Japan?

**Kiam:** We were in Japan, but she really meant American society. That has always stuck with me. Since then, I've been really critical and hyper-aware of the invisibility of Filipinos. Filipinos are the second-largest Asian population in the US, and yet there are hardly any Filipino restaurants and we have basically zero representation in the media. I've always wondered, "Why is that? Why is it that we kind of just disappear into the background of people's consciousness when we are so populous?" We are in every part of industry. We basically run the food service in the military. Filipinos are on every single cruise ship. We're everywhere and yet we're nowhere to be seen. When I talk about performance and taking up space and being in public, I'm always coming with that background in mind. I'm claiming space, claiming attention, and claiming my own humanity and presence in that space at that time.

**Nia:** Do you feel that being Filipino on stage is a political act—in that you're showing "I am here"?

**Kiam:** Very much so. For example, my video "Nostalgia" is a collage of different pop-cultural and political events that happened in the Philippines between 1985 and 1995, which is this timeframe that everyone's a little bit obsessed with right now.

**Nia:** Obsessed in the States, the Philippines, or both?

**Kiam:** In the US, specifically. I wanted to show a sampling of a similar aesthetic—you can tell that the videos are dated by the sound quality, the fashion, and the sound of the music. I wanted viewers seeing that video to feel this strange disconnect between something being really familiar but then completely foreign at the same time. That video piece is a contradiction in itself. When it's accompanied by the performance by Jerry Blossom[2], it's set up so that people are watching this video and then Jerry Blossom is in the audience, usually as the only Filipino there and the only one who gets what's being displayed on-screen. Jerry gets really excited and starts talking about the video in Tagalog, saying, "Oh, I remember that!" and trying to get people into it, like, "Hey, remember this? Oh, isn't that a great song? I love Imelda Marcos. She's got so many shoes." [*laughter*]

**Nia:** So it's kind of like an inside joke. You've created something that has nostalgic value only for you because you're the only person who understands it.

**Kiam:** Exactly. According to people who've seen the performance, it creates this strange disconnect where on the one hand, Jerry Blossom becomes kind of exotified, like, "Oh, look at this foreign person speaking." Then there's also the disconnect of the non-

---

[2] "Jerry Blossom is Kiam's alter-ego, a genderqueer Filipino femme-presenting persona who hails from an alternate post-queer, post-colonialist utopia/universe in which the Philippines is a world power." – IAmKiam.com

Filipino viewer trying to be a part of that art piece and yet feeling that they can't go there.

**Nia:** It kind of makes the viewer the "foreigner" because they're the one who doesn't understand what they're looking at?

**Kiam:** Exactly. In the video, there's a very small clip from a Mariah Carey video. My intent with that was to show that the Philippines were not a bubble—we had a lot of American pop culture influence. That was just as much part of our development in that time as anything else. That clip also gives the audience just that little, brief respite, like, "That's something I'm familiar with."

**Nia:** It's this brief moment of something you can hold onto that's familiar, and then it's right back to the stuff that you don't understand.

**Kiam:** Right. That's kind of how I try to operate with my performance in general—giving viewers an access point, but then keeping it personal also. In the personal is the political.

**Nia:** Earlier I talked about my interest in whether artists choose to let their audiences in or shut their audiences out, and you just described an example of a time when shutting your audience out was a very intentional political act. Do you feel in general like your desire for your work is for it to be accessible and understood? How much does it matter to you that your audience gets what you're trying to do or say with your pieces?

**Kiam:** I feel it is very important that my audience understands my message, but I also try to honor different people from different access points. It's a different conversation when I'm showing pieces to an art audience that is familiar with references or history or what it means to use mirrors in an art piece, versus someone just coming in and experiencing the visual impact of something. I try to acknowledge that people have different levels of access to my art and then give them enough information so that if they want to learn more that information is there. I never try—maybe it's part of my Asian upbringing, I don't know—but I try not to shove the intent on people, but rather say, "It's available if you want it."

**Nia:** It sounds like in your work there's something for everyone. There are things that maybe an art audience will have a better appreciation or understanding of than a non-art audience, and things that a queer audience of color will be able to take away from it that maybe a white or a straight audience won't.

**Kiam:** Exactly. I'd even want to say that these are not necessarily hierarchical access points, but rather different depths. I really believe that everyone looks for their reflection in other people, and that's why I love using mirrors in my artwork. My theory is that we always look at things or look at people to see what we see of ourselves reflected back. The more that we have in common, the more we are united with people, and the more we understand, the deeper that experience is. So of course I have a much closer affinity and a more loving energy towards other queer people of color because we do share more of that experience together.

This idea segues into my fashion line, Qiam. I put in my statement that I prioritize local queer people of color. That's who I really want to get my clothes onto because the way that the clothing line is going to operate is that pieces are all handmade for each person and made-to-order. I'm trying to have this dialogue and this transference of energy. Like, "I'm creating this for you. I'm performing this labor for you. Each of these stitches is for you."

**Nia:** It seems like that would make the clothing a lot more expensive, if it's custom-made for each individual.

**Kiam:** I haven't quite decided on the pricing yet. I'm trying to make it sustainable for me, of course—I'm trying to pay my rent and eat—but I'm also welcoming different forms of payment, like skill-sharing, gift exchange, or trading something else, where both parties can feel that they're benefitting.

**Nia:** Since you're focused on having your consumer base be local, does that mean the clothes will not be available to purchase online?

**Kiam:** Not necessarily. I welcome both modes of production. I do have patterns that I can use to make a bunch of clothing if I need to, and that clothing could be made available for a wider release. Each item of clothing is handmade with the intention of honoring individual bodies. It's an alternative to fast fashion, which is inherently capitalistic, colonialist, and binary-based.

**Nia:** Can you explain "fast fashion" for folks who might not be familiar with the concept?

**Kiam:** Fast fashion is really anything that you can find at a department store, anything that has multiples that are exactly the same—the clothing at places like H&M, Urban Outfitters, all the fashion outlets, really. The way the clothing is produced is very much mechanized and uses human labor as machinery, essentially. The way I understand fashion production to work, there's one worker doing one specific stitch at a time, and then it moves on to the next one—

**Nia:** Like an assembly line.

**Kiam:** Yeah. It's an assembly line. My goal with my brand is to not have that mechanized production, but rather to have the intention of making each piece one at a time, and to represent all of those people who are part of making that garment. In the same way that there's fast food and there's a chef-created gourmet dish, I consider my clothing to be like a gourmet dish. It's done with intention and with awareness of the type of body or the type of experience of the person who's going to wear it.

**Nia:** Is there anything that you'd like to talk about that we didn't get a chance to?

**Kiam:** I do welcome, of course, people from all over checking out my work. I'm making not just tank tops, but also jock straps and different accessories. My tagline is "Fashion tops, bottoms, and versatile accessories." With the jock straps, I'm making two models: one with a pouch and one with a triangular swatch of fabric, so that anyone can purchase one.

**Nia:** Why jock straps and tank tops?

**Kiam:** Tank tops, I feel, are one of the most basic articles of clothing because they can be unisex. They have a very basic form and are such versatile garments. You can layer a tank top over or under things, or you can wear it by itself. I make jock straps mainly because they use a smaller piece of fabric, so I can use the scraps from the tank tops to make them.

**Nia:** So you could have a matching tank top and jock strap?

**Kiam:** Yeah, you could. [*laughter*] And they're sexy! They really are. They're also just really simple pieces of clothing—three pieces of elastic and a swatch of fabric. That's all it is. I appreciate the simplicity and the sexiness of it. Jock straps have historically been for athletic use, and I feel like now they're for sexual use.

**Nia:** I'm sorry. I don't actually know what you're talking about.

**Kiam:** Well, jock straps have an elastic band, then a piece of fabric that covers the junk, and then two pieces of elastic, one on each side of the butt area. Jock straps really highlight the butt. They're really aesthetically pleasing in that way. [*laughter*] Also, people use it in sexual play. It's actually really common in gay male culture to see jock straps. Like, *everybody* has a jock strap.

I know some of my trans friends are interested in having a jock strap, and I thought it was unfair that all jock straps have the pouch, that they inherently make this shape where things are "supposed" to be. I saw some videos of trans guys wearing jock straps and saw that jock straps are not made for them, so I wanted to honor that experience. If someone wants to wear a jock strap, why shouldn't they be able to? That's why I'm making them for different audiences.

**Nia:** That's awesome. If people are interested in learning more about your work, they should go to iamkiam.com or iamkiam.tumblr.com.

**Kiam:** Yes. I have multiple websites—I have my photography website, I have my yoga website, I have my fashion website, I have my blog, and I have my art website.

**Nia:** I have that problem, too. I have, like, five Tumblrs and then another website and it's like, "There's got to be a better way to do this."

**Kiam:** Exactly. Multiple access points, multiple intentions. Whatever you're interested in, I'm here, and there's a direction.

Transcribed by Amirah Mizrahi

### Miss Persia and Daddie$ Pla$tik

**Miss Persia:** At the MOMA [Museum of Modern Art] in San Francisco one day, I just showed up in drag and worked all day. They were like, "Okay" and that led to jobs. Actually, MOMA hired me a few times.

**Nia King:** To do drag?

**Miss Persia:** Yeah, I was Matisse's *Woman with a Hat* for Pride two years ago and MOMA loved my work, so they flew me to LA. I was there for San Francisco Travel. I took a trolley bus from SF to LA. It made random stops and was just advertising San Francisco. I got to ride on a trolley bus all day, all over LA for two days from 6:00 in the morning to 6:00 in the evening in drag, in like one-hundred-degree weather. I was dying! [*laughter*]

I'm going to have a new job and my future boss used to be a drag king so she's like, "I can't wait to tell the kids that you do drag!" and I'm like, "I don't know, I'm scared!" [*laughter*] She's like, "You're going to have to do our fundraiser in drag," and I'm like, "Okay?"

**Nia King:** I guess the question is how do you capitalize on what you have? Or is "capitalize" a dirty word?

**Tyler Holmes:** It's appropriate and dirty. We're starving artists, literally. At some point it's like, "Okay, we'll play that show. Can you feed us? Can you give us tips? Because we are actually starving." I think we've gotten to the point where we don't necessarily ask for very much, but if we do need to ask, we will. I think that people are a little more receptive or they're paying more attention to what's happening. They're offering those kinds of things more because they appreciate what we do and they know that to get up there and perform, we have to be alive. [*laughter*]

**Nia King:** You said earlier that as an artist you're prostituting yourself?

**Vain Hein:** Yes.

**San Cha:** We are prostituting ourselves.

**Vain Hein:** We're all whores. When I said I was a whore earlier, I was kind of joking but kind of not.

**Nia King:** When you say you're "prostituting" yourself as an artist, what do you mean by that?

**Miss Persia:** Well, we're trying to seduce you into tipping us more. When I host an event, I go up to everyone and I'm like, "Hi, gorgeous, how are you? If you want to buy me a rum-and-diet, I wouldn't be opposed to that." [*laughter*] It's just like selling yourself.

I was talking to a man a few weeks ago and he was telling me how he put himself through college doing drag in Iowa because *there* they pay you. They pay you for performance. You do a number and they pay you at least a hundred bucks just for a number—and they tip. You walk out of there with hundreds of dollars in tips. He was like, "I moved to San Francisco and they were trying to tell me I was going to perform for exposure" and he did and he didn't get a free drink or any tips. In San Francisco, you have to *seduce* everyone.

**San Cha:** Yeah, I mean, I literally take my clothes off on stage.

**Tyler Holmes:** Me, too.

**Nia King:** It doesn't seem like there's any coercion involved.

**San Cha:** No!

**Tyler Holmes:** Well, there's positive sex work, too. Just because something is sex work doesn't mean I don't want to do it.

**Nia King:** Yeah, for sure. It's just that "sex work" and "prostituting yourself" have very different connotations. I feel like "prostituting yourself" implies that there's some element that you're not comfortable with, that you don't really feel good about, that you can't be your whole self.

**Tyler Holmes:** I think that's the thing that doesn't work for me. For me, selling out would be someone telling me that I can't say something queer, that I can't make a feminist statement—that would be like prostitution for me. Getting slutty, taking my clothes off, shaking my ass—I'm totally comfortable with that.

**San Cha:** In your way, though, in your way. It's not like, go over there, get waxed up, shave your everything, and—

**Tyler Holmes:** I mean, if someone was offering tips, girl, I don't know. I don't know.

**San Cha:** Yeah. [*laughter*]

**Tyler Holmes:** I *am* hungry…

**Nia King:** You mentioned before that feminism really informs your work—could you talk a little bit about how?

**Tyler Holmes:** I grew up with a single mother in a single-parent home. I feel like being in a single-parent home and coming from a domestic violence background and being queer all very much made me appreciate strong women and female characters. It made me understand and made me see firsthand that all that is feminine and all that is outside of gender boxes period is squashed or undervalued or disgraced or humiliated or destroyed.

Growing up in Marin County and having the opportunity to see a lot more fluid gender things and having a bit of an education on gender fluidity made me see that gender is really not a thing. Like, your assigned physical, biological sex is more of a thing and gender is like what you're wearing today. The term "drag" gets thrown around a lot with us. Vain has done drag before, and Miss Persia has done drag before, but San Cha and I don't do drag and we've been labeled drag performers, drag phantasms because we put on makeup.

**San Cha:** Not that we're not, but…

**Tyler Holmes:** We don't lip-sync…

**San Cha:** You can't hire us to go over there and lip-sync, like what you think a drag queen is going to do.

**Nia King:** I think people refer to it as drag because they don't know what to make of you.

**Vain Hein:** It's great, though.

**Tyler Holmes:** The term "drag" has become very confusing to me because no matter what I put on my body, whether it's boy clothes or girl clothes, it all feels like drag to me. It's like boy drag or girl drag—there's nothing neutral. I feel neutral to begin with. One of the most important messages that I can give people is that who you are is fine and we need to treat each other equally in all senses, especially regarding gender. Get the fuck out of my pants. Treat me like a person.

**San Cha:** People ask me all the time if I have a dick and I don't see why they'd want to know, unless they're trying to sleep with me. It's funny when people feel like it's an important question to ask me, especially when they don't know me. For people to really be that...*concerned*? For it to be that important that they have to ask me is very funny. It's just like, why does it matter? Are you going to treat me differently if I say "yes" or "no"?

**Nia King:** Can we talk about art school? I'm really interested to hear about your experience.

**Vain Hein:** As we were talking about earlier, we all in Daddie$ Pla$tik grew up in sort of dogmatic, religious, oppressive backgrounds. My dad was a born-again Christian when I was four or five. I was still at a fresh little young age. All of the things that were fed to me I took in and believed very deeply, but as I got older and hit puberty…I mean, it was always very obvious that I was queer even though I didn't have the language to talk about it and some of my family members didn't even want to address it. There was no dialogue about that in my family, especially not from my father. He told my mom he didn't want to address it because he thought that if he spoke to it, it would become reality.

Once I started hitting puberty and feeling sexual things, all of a sudden, everything else changed. All of a sudden, the things that were being told to me didn't make sense and they felt wrong. It didn't feel genuine. I felt lost. I was scared. I tried to get deeper into religion to suppress it, but it just felt worse and worse. My mom and my dad separated when I was very young. My mom saw that I was miserable and she decided to let me live with her for the final couple of years of high school and enrolled me in this charter art school. I think she knew that I was creative. I didn't really know it, but she knew.

She enrolled me, and I was just like some sort of phoenix. It actually happened in Phoenix, Arizona. [*laughter*] I was born there, but I lived with my father in Washington State and went back to Phoenix for this high school. Sort of like this phoenix from the ashes, I exploded with all this creative, queer craziness. Art really allowed me to do that, so I was like, "This is what I want to do."

There were a bunch of colleges that came during my senior year of high school. You know, "Come to our school! Come to our school! This is what you can do!"

**Miss Persia:** "It costs thirty thousand dollars!"

**Vain Hein:** Yeah, but they don't tell you that! [*laughter*] I was broke, but I still decided that art school was what I wanted to do and my mom was into it. I got there, and it took me a while to get a hold of what was actually happening. I realized that I was there strictly because they wanted my money and that they couldn't care less about me as a person or as an artist. There was no education on how to receive money as an artist—no classes on how to write grants, how to write a proposal. They just wanted my money and then on top of that I was realizing that the institution of art was very bigoted and geared towards white male domination. It made me so uncomfortable, but I felt like I had to finish art school. I had set myself a goal and I just wanted to complete it.

I left feeling like I learned a lot about myself over a really short period of time. I'm not sure I would have been able to do that elsewhere. I also learned what I didn't want in my life and sought out other things elsewhere and came across these lovely folks [Miss Persia and fellow Daddie$ Pla$tik members] a year later. In a nutshell, I just felt like art school was very racist and sexist and all of that bullshit.

**San Cha:** My dad would always say, "Why are you making music? You're not the daughter of a rich man." That understanding and attitude is because of institutions like art school.

**Vain Hein:** I was going to school with a bunch of kids who—

**San Cha:** Trust fund kids.

**Vain Hein:** Trust fund kids who were there because they thought it would be an easy 'A.' I was there because it was what I really wanted to do. Their artistic visions became a reality because they had money to do it, while I was literally making things out of nothing. I loved doing that, but things were picking up for other people that weren't happening for me because those other people had the means and I didn't.

**Miss Persia:** That's why I left SFAI [San Francisco Art Institute].

**Vain Hein:** I went there, too. You went for a year?

**Miss Persia:** Yeah, for a year. I did a post-bac in photography there and hated it. I didn't know about the financial woes of the school until I got there and I was already in debt. I lasted a year. The facilities were *horrible*. Before moving here, I had moved back home to LA and was going to East Los Angeles College where I was taking photo classes and everything was brand new— and this was East LA College! Then I came here and I was paying forty grand a year and the facilities were *busted*. Like Vain, I said,

"I'm going to do the one year, finish this, and see where I go from there." I will say I did meet some of the best teachers ever. What they lacked in facilities and resources and the horrible students, they made up for with really great teachers.

**Vain Hein:** Yeah, I met some really great mentors.

**Miss Persia:** It was really life-changing for me. I got to go to Ireland because of SFAI, so I can't totally hate on it, but I did feel tricked.

**Vain Hein:** I felt totally fooled.

**Miss Persia:** The teachers were trying to get me to continue with a master's and I was like, "Hell no!" [*laughter*] I was like, "You want me to be even more in debt and not have a job afterwards?" Because student loans, those don't go away. I'm like, "No, I can't, I can't."

**Nia King:** [*to San Cha*] You went to school for music?

**San Cha:** Yeah, it was at a four-year university. When I was in high school, I did this program called The Puente Project. It's an English class, but you have the same teacher for three years. You get put in an AP [Advanced Placement] class as a junior and as a senior. The program is really gearing you towards a four-year college. My freshman year, I didn't want to go to college, but they were like, "Private universities are what's going to give you more money and a four-year college is what you need to get to," so that's what I thought. I was going to college.

I went to St. Mary's College in Moraga, and I was going into it like, "I'm going be an international business major!" The first lecture I went to—they gave a lecture for freshmen or something—

somebody said that bachelor's degrees aren't even counting for that much anymore, so do what you love. I went straight out of there and I signed up for all the music classes.

They had a tiny, tiny music major population—there were only four or five of us in our class—but it was incorporated into a performing arts major, so I was a performing arts major with an emphasis in music. I was also totally in debt from two years there. After two years, I knew that I didn't belong there. It was a private school and there were a lot of really privileged kids. I was always broke. I didn't have money to eat out. Of course my friends would help me out, but after two years I couldn't do it any more and I transferred over to San Francisco State University where I had to retake all the music classes I had already taken and all the theory I had slaved over. It was so stressful. After a year at SF State, I dropped out and did music on my own.

**Nia King:** [*to Tyler Holmes*] You also went to an art high school?

**Tyler Holmes:** I went to a school called Marin School of the Arts. The first half of the day would be regular school and then there were two periods of art. My dream was to become a visual artist and installationist. I took painting and learned to stretch my own canvases and did things that seemed very expensive and very white to me. I got in based on the merit of my artwork—I turned in a portfolio—and I didn't learn until later that most people paid for it and somehow got in.

**Nia King:** They didn't have to submit a portfolio?

**Tyler Holmes:** No, people still submitted portfolios, but then their parents paid for them to attend, and I never paid a cent.

Vain and I feel like we had inverted experiences in the art high school department because I learned classical painting, how to use traditional colors and stretch my own canvas and all that stuff. I took creative writing, but every time I wanted to think outside of the box, it was very much restricted. I remember we did our self-portraits and mine looked like me. It was getting pretty nice, but I was bored just painting my face because I don't like painting. I hate it and I'd taken it for years.

Halfway through, by the time the portrait looked like me, I made myself into a zombie because I was bored and didn't want to try to paint the portrait as realistically as possible. At the end of the year I was like, "Where did my zombie painting go?" They were like, "Oh, we painted over it." I had a pretty harsh experience in that way because I wanted to think outside the box and do very conceptual art.

**Nia King:** They took your painting and painted over it?

**Tyler Holmes:** Gesso-ed right over it. It was a blank canvas.

**Miss Persia:** That's crazy!

**Tyler Holmes:** That sucked. I really did like that painting. I had a lot of experiences like that because I wasn't…The kids I was in school with had been taking art classes and had been drawing and doing all that stuff for a long time in a very classical sense where they had lessons and they had instructors. I had been drawing since birth, writing lyrics, and doing all sorts of creative things, but I had never painted before in my life in that conventional way. I just wanted to be involved in something artistic, and I didn't think that I could do music because I didn't know music and I thought that music was something for other people. The whole time I was in high school I was dabbling in music, but I felt very removed from it and very self-conscious about it, so I focused on visual art.

Toward the end of high school, I started to find a vein that worked for me. I did a lot of stencil work, a lot of big graffiti, and a lot of pop art because I like representational imagery. What we do as Daddie$ Pla$tik is pop art, kind of in the Andy Warhol sense—showing society or people what they are doing and offering conversation about that. Like "This is what's happening," like with "Google Google Apps Apps." San Francisco is being gentrified. People want to be white. We don't want to be white, that's not a true statement for us, but…

**San Cha:** I feel like, growing up in a mostly Latino, Filipino, and Vietnamese community, a lot of people *did* want to be white.

**Tyler Holmes:** Yeah, because white people have money and can afford to live their lives.

**Vain Hein:** People wear contacts to make their eyes blue.

**San Cha:** People brag about being lighter or they talk shit about people who are darker. It happens with our own communities.

**Miss Persia:** I'm the darkest in my family, so I was always called the dark one—el prieto—in a put-down way. I am dark. I'm not *that* dark, but between my sisters and my parents, I'm the darkest. I have other darker relatives, too, and they got a lot of shit for it. I was able to cope with it, but not everyone is able to cope with it. Even now, my sister stays out of the sun purposefully because she's the lightest of all three of us—and that's one of the things she prides herself on. She's like, "I'm the lightest of you all" and I'm like, "I don't care! People pay to be tan like me, so get some sense!"

**Tyler Holmes:** Every canon of beauty is oppressive and through globalization, through the spread of American culture as *the* culture, through things like Hollywood that teach you that to be happy, you need to be a thin, white, blonde woman who attracts a wealthy—

**San Cha:** A Paris Hilton.

**Tyler Holmes:** A Paris Hilton, who attracts a wealthy man who basically pays you for sex, because women aren't supposed to like sex.

**San Cha:** And buys you with a diamond ring.

**Tyler Homes:** Who purchases you with a diamond ring.

**Miss Persia:** I need a diamond ring! [*laughter*]

**Tyler Holmes:** I would be pawning that shit tomorrow! [*laughter*] Going back to religion, something I always dealt with was my father being very religious and saying, "You need to do this! You need to do that!" I'd always be like, "How are you telling me how to live my life when you do terrible things?"

**Vain Hein:** There's a Bible verse that's like, before you take the speck out of your brother's eye, take the log out of yours.

**Tyler Holmes:** "He who casts the first stone..."

**Vain Hein:** I wish that I could remember; I wish that I could tell you which Book that came from... [*laughter*]

**Tyler Holmes:** John!

**Vain Hein:** But the fact that I know that quote alone is ridiculous.

**San Cha:** Well, we all grew up on it. I was singing in the church choir from the time I was twelve. I was playing an instrument from the time I was ten. That all developed into this whole Goth San Cha kind of shit. I was up there in miniskirts singing with the choir and all of my aunts would be telling my mom, "You let her go up there like that?" and she'd be like, "Why are you looking at her? You should be praying." [*laughter*]

**Tyler Holmes:** Praying is not what I'd like to tell people to do. I would be like, "Be critical of the things that are around you." That's what they want you to do—"they" in quotation marks—they want us to fight each other over bullshit. Fight each other over "You're queer, you're different than me, you're brown, you're different than me," whereas we don't notice that the actual problems are that institutions fuck us to death. Constantly. All of us. In every way.

**Nia King:** So, the religious background—is that part of why you guys are so explicitly sexual and kind of obscene?

**San Cha:** Not the only reason, but…

**Vain Hein:** A large part of it.

**San Cha:** I mean, my brothers and sisters aren't the same way.

**Vain Hein:** No. [*laughter*]

**San Cha:** They went through the same thing I did, but we, for some reason, grew up with a different urge. I don't know why.

**Vain Hein:** We're all different people, but I happen to be the one in my family where something snapped. [*laughter*] I'd say it was in large part due to feeling oppressed, feeling like I wasn't allowed to feel the things I felt, like being attracted to men—oh my god!

**Tyler Holmes:** Heaven forbid.

**Vain Hein:** It does make the element of sexuality in my work more extreme because I'm pushing against religion.

**Tyler Holmes:** Body image is a big part of it for me. I've been a bigger person and a smaller person. For me, it's about wanting to push positive sexuality and body acceptance. I've always felt that there's nothing wrong with sex and there's nothing wrong with our bodies and that the way they're hidden and restricted is ridiculous. I think that it comes out of me naturally, just being free in that way. I think that people take it as extreme because you're supposed to be covered up or whatever. To us, it's not a big deal.

**San Cha:** A funny thing I would think of at church: I'd be like, being silent and being still and stuff when everyone was sitting down, because you have to turn and listen to the priest, and I would always think, "What would happen if I just threw myself on the ground and started screaming?" [*laughter*] I thought of that so many times.

**Miss Persia:** And now you do it all the time! [*laughter*] Everywhere we go! Scaring the tourists and shit.

**San Cha:** I thought, "What's stopping me from doing that? What's actually stopping me from doing that? Nothing. Just me trying to be respectful…of what?" At that time, I was already questioning religion and everything that people were telling me.

**Vain Hein:** I remember that my "aha!" moment was when there was a guest preacher. He was on tour and he had gotten everyone in the church into hysteric holy laughter on their backs, rolling around like [*imitates laughter*], and I was trying to do it, and then I realized, "I'm *trying* to do this. It's not really happening, and all these people are just bullshitting." [*laughter*] Everyone was so involved in that bullshit, rolling around on the floor, looking like dumbasses.

I got up and left and nobody even noticed. I just walked around. I walked into the woods as far as I could go and back until church was over. Nobody even realized I had left until later. I just thought it was the most insane, scary thing I had ever seen. I realized for the first time that all of those people lying on the ground were completely brainwashed because I had been faking it, too. I swear, I saw a woman like [*high-pitched laughter and panting*].

**Tyler Holmes:** Oh my god.

**Vain Hein:** I know!

**San Cha:** I want to go there!

**Vain Hein:** You would have been right at home!

Transcribed by Emily Scowley

## Virgie Tovar

**Virgie Tovar:** When I was twenty-four or twenty-five and working in radio, I was always shying away from making things about me. I was always like, "Let's have a guest. Let's interview somebody. Let's talk about something else." My mentor at the station, who was a man, would be like, "No, let's talk about *you*." That's something that women are not trained to do, especially women of color and queer women of color. How many people come up to us and say, "No, we want to hear about *you*, this is about *you*, let's bring it back to *you* now"? [*laughter*] I've had these opportunities where I've come into contact with people who have encouraged me to see myself as somebody whose narrative is really important and interesting, and I see my job in a lot of ways as being to do the same for other people who are like me.

**Nia King:** Can you talk a little bit about your experience in higher education and how that might have contributed to the career you have now?

**Virgie:** I experienced a lot of opposition in graduate school. Most of the faculty was not particularly supportive of my work. There was nobody doing work that was similar to mine. The advisor who ended up signing off on my thesis tried to dump me three weeks before the signing-off was supposed to happen. There was a person in my program who took my thesis idea. I shared it with her and she took it within a week. Everybody pretended it hadn't happened. When I brought it up, I was sort of ignored. I didn't understand how something I had clearly stated as a research interest all of a sudden became hers and nobody said anything. I felt really angry. I felt really silenced. I felt really aggravated.

I was told in graduate school that I was among colleagues, that I was in a place to share knowledge, and I took that at face value. I think a lot of people who don't know the hustle that is racism—a lot of us take that shit to heart, but it's not real, it's not right, and it's not true. The truth of the matter is that when you're in graduate school, it is not about being collegial and it is not about having a "marketplace of ideas." If you have a good idea, you need to be extremely politically- and strategically-minded and you better be prepared for somebody to take that shit, and you better figure out how you're going to deal with that when it happens, because it's very possible that your idea is either going to get taken or shat upon. You're going to have to pick yourself up and do the work of being your own number-one advocate.

People of color, women, and women of color—we have not been taught to have the confidence that you need to really succeed in a world like academia. We're afraid of failure, we're afraid of what it means to get feedback even, because our understanding of our capacity is so limited and that holds us back from taking challenges. Whereas when you look at white males in academia, those men have a wellspring of confidence that we don't have. When they fail, that doesn't hit them to the core. That doesn't debilitate them. They think, "I'm still awesome. This might have happened, but that person is stupid. That person doesn't know what they're talking about. That person doesn't know shit." That's the attitude that I think we need to have and that I'm building up now in my own career.

I was told by a professor that I didn't have the intellectual rigor to complete her course and for her to say that to somebody…it was so heartbreaking at the time. I ended up going into anger management. I ended up going to the health services provided for free at San Francisco State University. I ended up talking to a therapist. I was having all these problems. I had never felt more like I was losing my mind. One of the therapists was an older woman of color. We were talking about my experience in graduate school and she said, "You don't know the game that you're playing." It was so intense in that moment to have this incredible intimacy with somebody who was an elder, who was a mentor in that moment, who broke it down for me and kept it real when she could have decided to be professional and distant and indifferent. She told me that academia is a game of whiteness and if you're not white, you don't know the stakes. You don't know the game. You don't know the moves and you've got to figure out how to survive, knowing that you cannot be authentic in those spaces.

In academia, I've learned concrete tools, like how to write well, how to write an essay in a way that will get it accepted to something, how to fill out applications, how to talk to people, how to have a meeting, but I was also taught all of these other skills, too—how to navigate sexism, how to navigate racism, how to support somebody who's going through the same thing you are. Those are indispensable tools for me as an activist and an artist.

**Nia:** You mentioned that you wrote your first book when you were twenty-four. How did you get your first book deal?

**Virgie:** You know, it's the funniest story. This is totally heteronormative hour. [*laughter*] When I was working in radio, one of my assignments was to go to events and cover them. One event came up and the station was like, "Go cover this." It was a flirting workshop in San Francisco at the Good Vibrations store on Polk Street. I was like, "Well, I'm pretty good at flirting, but I'm happy to go see what's up." It was this woman—I don't remember her name, but she does these empowerment, flirting, flirt-for-love, flirt-for-success kinds of workshops. She's kind of like a guru. She was offering this one-day intensive workshop, so I go in there…

Let me back up and say that I had it in my mind, and I had put it out to the universe as a known fact—I was like "Universe, I'm going to write a book before I turn twenty-five." In my head that was the truth. It hadn't happened yet, but it was truth as far as I was concerned—"I don't know how this is going to happen, but this *is* going to happen." I feel like that's kind of the person I've been, somebody who's like, "This is my passion, this is what I want, and it is done because I *say* it is done." I think this is the power-femme top thing…

I go to this flirting workshop and there are a few cute boys. There are, like, three boys and I'm like, "Hmm, three." I call it "scoping the fuckability." I scoped the fuckability—there were three prospects. I kind of had an order in my head.

During the first break, my second choice came up to me and he started talking. He was kind of lathering it up, but he didn't close the deal. He was like, "I'd really like you to come teach a class at such and such, you're really interesting, blah blah blah." You know, great, he teed it up, but he did not close the deal. I was like, "Okay, that's cool." What I loved was that choice number one was standing right behind him, kind of hovering to see what he'd do.

Halfway through the class, right before the lunch break, we had an eye contact exercise. The woman is like, "Okay, I want there to be two lines, and I want you to sustain eye contact for one minute." I was partnered with choice number one. We made eye contact really intensely. We were still looking at each other and the woman said, "Okay, it's time for lunch, you have thirty minutes." He walks right up to me, takes my hand and says, "I have to take you to lunch." [*laughter*] We go to lunch and he's like, "What do you do besides looking like a goddess all the time?" We're bantering, really flirtatious, and I'm like, "You know, right now I'm doing radio, but I'm also going to be writing a book." I was like, "I'm writing a book and it's going to be published before I turn twenty-five." He's like, "That is so funny. I'm actually a publisher." I was like, "Okay, yeah, that makes sense." [*laughter*]

There's a lot of chemistry. After the class, we take a cab to my apartment. We start making out and right before he pulls my shirt up, I say, "If my choice is between dating you and you being my publisher, I choose publisher." [*laughter*] This is me being a total career person—career is number one for me in a lot of ways, for better or for worse. He was like, "I think we can do both." I was like, "Okay."

Within a week, we'd drawn up an agreement. He offered to basically fund the project. He was like, "I'm not going to be able to pay you, but I'll pay for everything and whatever money you make from the book and from sales of the book in-person, you can keep that money." It was one of those situations where I didn't get an advance, but otherwise it was a no-lose situation. Within three months I had finished the book—it was already in my head, you know. It became *Destination DD: Adventures of a Breast Fetishist with 40DDs*.

**Nia:** I'm interested in your experience of writing a book versus editing a book.

**Virgie:** When I set out to edit *Hot & Heavy: Fierce Fat Girls on Life, Love & Fashion*, my thought was, "I know all of these ferocious fat bitches who are so amazing and so fierce, and I'm going to ask them how they became so fierce." I thought the stories were going to be funny and almost like a romantic comedy. What I found was that the stories were really, really, really complicated, and a lot of them were not sunshine and puppies and romantic comedy shit. It was serious, intense shit. I realized that my understanding of "fierce" had been totally one-dimensional—I only saw the shiny parts. I didn't see what went into what it meant to be fierce.

Now that the book has come out and I've talked to people about it, it blows my mind to hear people's impressions of what this word means. I remember once I was giving a lecture and the professor had assigned the introduction of my book to the students to read. She asked everybody to go around and say what they felt like the word "fierce" meant. Everybody had all these different answers that were really good, then there was this one queer person of color and they said, "Fierceness is armor." It was like, "Oh, shit." It still gives me chills to remember those words.

The word "fierce" has been absorbed into our culture and it comes very much from queer-people-of-color community, queer-people-of-color history. When you think about queer people of color, especially femmes of color, the amount of resilience that is needed to survive in a world that is constantly bombarding their identities and their bodies is incredible, and then to turn it into this thing where it looks fashionable and looks stylish and looks sexy and looks effortless—that shit is not effortless!

There was a moment where I was worried that when I turned in the book my editor was going to be like, "This is really depressing" or like, "This isn't what we talked about." I decided to go with telling the story and being honest with the story.

I actually talk about this in the introduction to the book, having that moment where I had to grow the fuck up as a writer and an editor because I was now responsible for a bunch of people's stories. There was so much going on. It was so clear to me that for some of the contributors, it was the first time they'd told their story. For some of them it was very, very vulnerable stuff they were sharing with me.

**Nia:** How did you get this second book deal?

**Virgie:** It's another sort of longish story—I apologize. [*laughter*] I knew about Seal Press in Berkeley because when I was working in radio, we used to book guests through them. They were in my head. I had just kind of gotten it in my head that these were the people I wanted to work with.

I had been in a long-distance relationship with a New Zealander. I had been working as a sex educator and then had quit my job and moved to New Zealand for five months. It was just one of those things where you're in another country, and you've just left this job: your heart is open, your spirit is open, your brain is open to all these different things. I remember I went on a trip to the Cook Islands, which are in the middle of the Pacific—you know what, I left out a part...

Back up a year before that: I had a contract working in tourism and one of the benefits of the contract was that you would be flown to all these different places for meetings, and sometimes you could be flown to local areas before your contract started. That particular year, I was in Boston right before I was going to be doing a contract in New York and New Jersey. I was in Boston and I was in this totally spiritually-elevated place. I just felt so good and so full and whole and complete, and I remember asking the universe in that moment, "Where am I headed? Where is this going?" This thought was just introduced into my head: "You are going to be part of the fat movement."

I had not done any organizing around fatness. I had read a few articles. I didn't even remember having read them. I realize now in retrospect, looking at the course readers I read in college, that I had read fat activism articles from several years ago, but I was not part of the movement. I didn't even know there was a movement at all.

But this thought was introduced into my head—"You're going to do this fat movement thing"—and I was like, "Okay, well, how do I do that?" The answer was "Just breathe." That was the answer: just get up and breathe. That's always the answer, no matter what—just get up and breathe. Time will tell. After that happened, I was like, "Alright, I'm just going to chill then because this is just going to happen with or without my knowledge or consent."

A while passes, a year maybe. I'm in New Zealand and I go to the Cook Islands. I'm writing wishes in the sand. I'm by myself and I write in the sand, "Fatties of the world unite!" which had been the name of a blog post that a friend had asked me to write right before I went to New Zealand. She said, "I'm doing a project on body image and I'd really like you to write for it. Will you write a post for this website we're making?" I was like, "Sure," so I wrote "Fatties of the World Unite." It was basically a rant about fat life and how fat life can be fucked up because people are fucked up about fat. It was about sex and men and all kinds of stuff. A lot of people really liked it. It really resonated with a lot of people.

When I came back to New Zealand, there was just a fire lit under my ass. I wrote a proposal in three days and sent it in from New Zealand to Berkeley, to Seal Press. It was for *Fatties of the World Unite*. I wrote the first two chapters. I wrote the introduction and another chapter. I had a table of contents, I had the concept, everything—all the things that were required.

By the way, just a little tidbit for people who are interested in submitting proposals: A lot of publishers who publish nonfiction will have the submission guidelines on their website so you can just follow those and submit a cold submission. You don't have to have an agent. Another little tidbit is that if you write nonfiction, you don't need an agent. If you write fiction, you need an agent.

I get an email back two months later from the Senior Editor

Brooke Warner, a woman I hugely respect who was at Seal Press then. She was like, "I really like your voice. This is a manifesto. This is really unusual nowadays. There are not many of those." She was like, "I don't know if this is going to make it past this point, but I just want to let you know that you have a voice and this is good." In that moment, as a young woman of color who didn't have a ton of confidence about her work, those words were huge to me.

The proposal didn't make it past the marketing team. They were like, "This is not going to reach the audience." At the time, the book was only about fat sex and fat sexuality. They basically said, "It won't be able to reach your market," which can mean a lot of things, but in this case meant "We don't know that it's going to be able to sell," because at the time fat issues hadn't really hit yet. It wasn't really a huge thing in academia yet and the big plus-sized fashion explosion hadn't happened yet—this all predates that.

I go to graduate school. I end up studying fat girls, doing my whole degree on fat women of color, queering the feminine. As I'm finishing up my degree, I send an email to Brooke. I say, "Brooke, I don't know if you remember me, but I'm the one who wrote *Fatties*. I'm the one who did that thing about fat. I don't know that I want to go through the whole submission process again like that; but if there's any interest in the work, let me know, and I'm willing to do whatever work you want me to do behind that." I was like, "I think now is the time"—that was what I said because after I'd done research, in the two years that had passed since the rejection, I felt like there had been this huge cultural shift. Brooke wrote back and was like, "I agree. I think it's the time, too. If you're willing to expand the idea beyond sex, I think that we can move forward on this. I want it to be more than that. I want it to be about all aspects of life as a fat girl."

I think she actually had a better, more complex idea than I'd had, a bigger vision than I'd had, and that was how *Hot and Heavy: Fierce Fat Girls on Love, Life & Fashion* became what it was. I was not demoralized by the initial rejection and I really took her at her word. I think what she really said in that first email where she was like, "We can't move forward" was "Right now isn't the time." A project can evolve. A project can be wrong at one time and right at another time. To be passionate is to have confidence in this thing, to ride it through and to be like, "This is going to come into the world one way or another." I'm really excited that the book came through Seal Press and I'm really excited that it came to fruition the way it did.

**Nia:** Where do you want to go from here?

**Virgie:** I don't know where it's going from here, and I think there's this element of surrender that I just have to realize is part of my life. I feel like every time I haven't just surrendered and just given in to what my body was telling me, things have gotten off-balance. I would love to continue to write. I would love to continue to create books, to continue to become an increasingly visible public intellectual figure. I seek to innovate that space between the public and the academy and to carve out a true space for public intellectuals.

Another ambition I have is to work in collaboration with people who are going to create infrastructure around opportunities for people of color, fat people, queer people, women—people I see in my community who I talk to all the time and they're broke as a joke, you know?

On one hand, I believe in a fairly modest lifestyle. I believe you don't need more than what you need, but at the same time, I believe that we have these moments of delicious food or delicious art or delicious travel or whatever, and I believe there can be beauty in those things and that people deserve those things as well. I'd like to see more people in my life not having to live paycheck-to-paycheck or even worse than that. I want to get to the point where I can leverage my projects or my name or whatever to get those things for people, to pay people and to increasingly see artists get paid.

I also see myself being part of a movement of demanding payment. I have been toying with the idea of creating a website where people pledge not to work for free and not to expect others to work for free. It's obviously a symbolic pledge—there's not going to be anybody knocking down your door if you don't follow it—but it becomes this thing and you could see all of these other people who have agreed to do this and how important this work is. When we don't pay artists, we sentence ourselves to a life where there won't be art by people of color, by queers, by women, and we know that it's struggle and critique and understanding and resilience that creates fantastic art. When the people who are experiencing those things aren't creating work, we lose things as a culture. We lose things as a species.

I want to see art that fucking rocks my world. I want to see art that makes me cry. I want to see art that makes me think. I know who's making that art and they're not getting paid. That means they're not going to be able to continue to make that shit, and that's not a life that I want to be a part of. Paying artists ends up being this reinvestment in a future I want to see.

**Nia:** How do you measure your success as an artist or a writer?

**Virgie:** That's a really complicated question. I have to admit that there is a big part of it that's measured by feedback from people who I consider experts or who are renowned in the field. Some of it has to do with money. A big part of my feelings of success comes from those kinds of affirmations that are very traditional.

Other affirmations of success are when I'm in a room full of queer people, people of color, trans people, women—does my message resonate with them? Are they coming up to me and saying, "I felt safe in this moment" or "I felt vindicated" or "I felt like I wasn't crazy" [*laughter*] or whatever? Are those folks coming to me? Are those folks engaging with my work?

There's also that internal barometer, that emotional knowledge inside my body—like, does this feel gross? Does this feel right? What kind of concessions am I making? Are they worth it? When you're doing anything—and this is where I feel like a lot of times artists can get demoralized or confused—once a project becomes funded or once a project becomes collaborative, you're not the only person who's responsible for the product and that can be daunting. I think a lot of people are afraid of what that would look like—"What would it look like to make a concession around this issue?" The answer to the question is…you know the answer to the question. Only you can answer that question—what's at stake is different for different people. My body tells me what concessions I'm willing to deal with and which ones I'm not.

I also measure success by who's drawn to me. What kind of people want to be friends with me? What kind of people want to collaborate with me? It's exciting for me right now because I feel like those people are all fucking high-quality, amazing, kick-ass, brilliant, inspiring people.

Here's something I feel like artists or people in general might find useful: Think about your time as something you can monetize. For example, if there's an organization that asks you to donate your time and your performance, you put a dollar amount on that time or that performance and you ask yourself, "If I had that dollar amount, would I give it to them?" If the answer is "yes," then donate that time, donate that performance. If the answer is "no," then don't.

Transcribed by Deelie Ree Jones

## Julio Salgado

**Julio Salgado:** It took me like nine-and-a-half years to graduate, but I finally graduated. In 2010, the year that I graduated, all this action started happening. The way that the media was covering it, they would show up, take a picture, write their story, get their paycheck, and move on. There was no depth to a lot of the stories, there was no analysis. No asking, "Why were the students doing it?" It was just about "illegal aliens trying to get free rides." The media was still calling us "illegals."

I was like, "Well, we need to document this, but it has to be from our voice. We are the ones who should be documenting all this stuff." For me, art was the way to do it, through posters and imagery that paid homage to what we were doing.

As I continued to create more work about being undocumented, I noticed that the narrative was "I'm an American. I am a good American. I am perfect. Accept me." I felt like it was a lot of asking for forgiveness. While I understand the political reasons behind this narrative, it's a pain to show other people that we are "just like you." The government hasn't asked for forgiveness from the people who have to come to this country, which is this country's fault. And nobody's perfect. For me, it became about saying that and about showing that we're not perfect.

There was one instance where one of the deportations that we were stopping was for somebody who had a DUI [Driving Under the Influence]. A lot of organizations were not taking those cases. They were like, "No. Those cases show that immigrants are bad for this country." It was like, "No! We are human." There's a big rate of depression and suicide among undocumented folks who take to alcohol. This case was a way to show these complex identities.

Documented or undocumented, people have to cope in different ways. That's not saying, "Oh, you should go ahead and drink and drive." It's not about that. It's about showing that we all make mistakes. It took folks taking on those cases—other undocumented folks specifically. DREAMactivist.org has been doing amazing work trying to stop deportations and trying to take on those cases that nobody really wanted to take because they put undocumented students in a different light, not in a positive light—this "perfect immigrant" image—that the Democrats or the paid organizers want to show.

I made that image with the student giving the middle finger after there was this bill in Florida. They were trying to pass the DREAM [Development, Relief, and Education for Alien Minors] Act without offering attending college as a route to legal status, just enlisting in the Army. They were like, "If you join the Army, then you can *try* to get papers." I was like, "Fuck that! Hell, no!" I'd rather stay undocumented or move to another country. The US is not the whole world. For me, it took a while to be brave enough to critique this country because for many years you're told you do not have the right to do that because you've been given a chance to be here without papers. I'm still coming to terms with doing that and using art to show that our identities as undocumented immigrants are complex.

I feel that my politics and the way that I think have definitely evolved from "Look, I'm a good student! I have a degree! I'm good" to "Fuck that! We are more than that. We are more than Social Security. We are complex human beings."

**Nia King:** Yeah. I'm glad that you're pushing that conversation. I feel like a lot of times when you're fighting for rights or fighting for acceptance, there's such a strong push to assimilate and to say that you're perfect, so saying "No, we're not, and that's okay" seems like a very risky thing to do.

**Julio:** Yeah. The way that my politics have evolved and shifted is because of the work of hella radical undocumented folks. There's this activist, who's also an amazing blogger and amazing writer, named Prerna Lal. I *love* her and the way that she's constantly challenging what it means to be undocumented through her writing, through her activism. Folks like her have made a huge difference in my life, in the sense of "Oh my god. What she's saying makes total sense." That's *how* my politics have evolved and changed. It's not something like, "Oh, you know, my art is making me realize it." No, *they're* making me realize shit. It just so happens that I can draw and make these images that are being created out of the conversation that has evolved.

That's not to say that because you don't agree with me I don't respect you. Today [May 19th] is Malcolm X's birthday, and I saw this image that somebody posted with something like "Don't hate somebody because they're not at the point of their life that you are. You are thinking this way because you learned this." Some folks don't have access to certain readings. I think it's important to have folks who are fighting and lobbying, but for me it's like, what about us and what we can do? Why put all these hopes on politicians and people who are doing this for their careers? How are we helping our communities? I definitely think that because of people like Prerna, I've evolved in my views. I'm very thankful for those folks.

**Nia:** When you describe the split in the undocumented activist community between assimilationist and radical or anti-assimilationist folks, it's hard for me not to make parallels between the LGBT community—the "We're just like you, we want to get married and join the military" versus the "Fuck all that" type of queers. Do you see a relationship there?

**Julio:** Of course! I think it's about evolving in the way we think. Again, I was like, "I'm an American citizen. I belong here." I think that getting papers is important—it's good—but we put *all* this importance on trying to get papers. Like I mentioned before, once I get my papers, that is not going to change the way people think if we don't change the culture. I can get my green card tomorrow and somebody who's an anti-immigrant person is still going to think I don't belong here. Latinos or brown folks who are US citizens and encounter those folks get the same shit, so it's not just about getting papers.

It's the same thing with gay marriage. If people want to get married, go for it. We have that conversation. My partner is on that ship, so I understand the importance of marriage. We shouldn't have to get married in order to have the same rights. I shouldn't have to do that to be able to see my partner in the hospital if something happens to them. We need to change what we give importance to.

At the same time, again, I understand why folks are fighting for that. I think any advancement is a positive advancement, but it's not just about that. I always wonder if, when the undocumented or the "DREAMers" get their papers because of the DREAM Act and start getting into politics, they are going to bring immigration policy back to what it is now, because a lot of the laws now are being pushed by folks who were at one time oppressed or at one time part of a community that was oppressing them.

Case in point: what happened at the Marriage Equality rally at the Supreme Court [March 2013]. The Human Rights Campaign folks were not letting trans folks or undocumented people speak publicly at the rally. It's like, how hypocritical! It just shows that once you go into this political bubble, you think that you're going to change shit, but you're going into the same thing, the same bullshit. There have got to be other ways. I think people have tried to imagine different ways.

Art is what I feel gives us some sort of ability to imagine different things, and that's where I'm trying to come in. We need to change that culture, change that way of thinking. Sometimes people might be like, "Ah, that's just a poster. It doesn't matter." But maybe somebody might see it and connect it to their beliefs. It happened to me—it happened to me in reading somebody's story, reading some radical ideas. I thought, "Damn, that's possible!" So I hope that happens.

But I definitely see that parallel of trying to assimilate. How do we not have to constantly beg others to accept us for who we are? Fuck everybody! I don't care. If you don't want to accept me, oh, well. [*laughter*] My grandma doesn't accept me. My grandma is a hardcore Baptist churchgoer. But she's my grandma. I love her. If she doesn't accept me, I don't care—I still love her. I'm going to be happy with me, and that's the important thing. You have to be happy with yourself and find some sort of healing in this craziness of a world.

**Nia:** You were talking about how people might say, "Oh, it's just a poster." I've been thinking about the relationship between art and activism. I went to art school, very briefly, [*laughter*] and found that it was a really hostile space for talking about politics. People had this idea of art—pure art—as existing just for art's sake and not really saying anything, which I had a *very* difficult time with. Sometimes with activist organizations, too, I find that the value of art is not really appreciated or understood as a tool for political struggle. Is that something you've come across in your work as an artist and activist?

**Julio:** There are definitely folks who feel that in order to make change you need to be on the streets, physically there. I agree that there's only so much you can do with online activism, but if nobody else knows about what's happening out there on the streets, and if you feel that that's the only way...

When there's money involved, I think a lot of times that's when it gets weird. As artists, we have to eat and pay rent. I don't really make a lot of money from my art. I work with an organization that's for art, but I don't sit around and make art all day because it doesn't work like that. There's all this money going into movements from foundations that are trying to figure out a way to—I don't want to say "capitalize" on this, but...the nonprofit bubble can be weird and awkward. [*laughter*] Imagine if that money were to go into creating more art.

Sometimes I wish I could have more money so that I could give these posters to folks because they're like, "How can I get more posters?" and I'm like, "Shit. I don't have the budget to print a bunch of posters. I wish I could." I think that's why my criticism is "Well, you nonprofits have this money to spend. Why don't you spend it on the art or creating more stuff?" People are visual. I don't think art is more important than on-the-ground organizing—I think both things are important—but we have to find ways of working together.

At the end of the day, people are stuck in their ways. "No, my way is the way that's going to work and yours is just wasting your time." I'm going to continue to respect you as an activist, and I'm going to continue to do what I'm doing but I'm not going to get mad at folks who feel that art is not as important, especially when I see that they're carrying a poster or sharing some of the images.

I'm still learning how the culture of art is important because it took me a while to even say that I'm an artist. I took two semesters of art classes and I was like, "No, I'm not an artist." As brown people, our parents don't really—I mean, my parents were very supportive of me being creative, but I know other folks whose parents were like, "No, that's not a real job. You need to get a job that really will pay the bills." It's a lot of learning and showing folks that art can be a good tool.

I hear folks who are like, "Art is not going to stop somebody's deportation." I'm going to continue to do what I have to do because this is what I know how to do. I can't organize something because I'm not the most organized person in the world, but I'm going to come in and be like, "How can I help?" because at the end of the day, I could be in that position of almost getting deported and I want to know that there's going to be somebody there who's going to have my back and help in case something happens to me, my family, or my friends.

**Nia:** You mentioned the pressure to get a job that pays the bills. How do you pay the bills? What do you do for a living?

**Julio:** I work at a nonprofit. [*laughter*] I work with Favianna Rodriguez and we collaborate on a lot of work. Favianna has really been my mentor. She teaches me a lot.

**Nia:** What's the organization?

**Julio:** I work with CultureStrike. My role at CultureStrike—because I know what it's like to be undocumented and to try to be an artist—is to bring in more undocumented artists to show their work. A lot of the time people are like, "Oh, Julio, you're like the only artist in the movement." No, I'm not. There are other folks who do amazing work. Like, they're freaking awesome! There are a lot of young folks. I used to be where they are now, like, "No, I'm not an artist, I don't want to show my work," so I really want to promote other undocumented folks who are artists. From writing to photography, there's all this talent.

A lot of the time it's just New York and LA that get the cultural things, but we forget about the in-betweens, especially the southern states, where there's no access because people are just so caught up in "Let's try to pass this bill." CultureStrike's goal is to bring in the art, bring in the artists, and have this network of folks to work with each other. We just did it in Los Angeles at the May Day event. Favianna has the butterflies—that's her thing right now—she's using butterflies to show that migration is beautiful. People have been using butterflies in their art for many years. Favianna has said it's not her idea, that she's just using them to represent migration.

I think one of the most popular uses of the symbol of the butterfly was when César Maxit created this butterfly that says "migrant" and has two fists in the wings. That was used for the UndocuBus, a bus we took from Arizona to DC for the Democratic National Convention. The butterfly was our symbol, so Favianna worked with César, saying, "How can we continue to use that butterfly symbol to push for migration?"

I'm helping Favianna with the "Migration Is Beautiful" campaign. We have a letter that other well-known artists have signed. We have people like REM, Tom Morello—folks who are dope and have this following. A lot of the time as activists we live in this bubble. We think that everybody knows what's happening, and that's not the case. There are people who have no idea what "undocumented" is or what it's like, or who say, "What do you mean 'undocumented'? You mean 'illegals'?" Or they have this idea that immigration is bad.

People have criticized the "Migration Is Beautiful" campaign. They're like, "Migration is not beautiful. Migration is actually ugly. People come here because they're forced." And that's true, those things happen. My thing is, how can we change that idea of people thinking, "We have to call out that migration can be horrible"? We need to honor ourselves and show ourselves that we're beautiful creatures, but I understand both sides of the criticism.

I think about people who have never been in a room with undocumented folks. That is where the other artists who have a bigger following come in, to educate their folks. So far we've gotten a really cool response. But again, we need to continue to go beyond that idea of "Try to accept me, I'm an American." That's part of my job with CultureStrike, in addition to expanding the use of culture and art.

I also do commission gigs on the side and I try to keep drawing. I'm always trying to figure out ways to collaborate with other folks who have amazing ideas. I'm really excited because I'm working on a piece with Mia McKenzie for her blog *Black Girl Dangerous*. That's another site I read where I'm just amazed by the ideas. I work with other folks, other communities. A lot of times we get stuck in the Latin@ immigration community.

A lot of the side projects I have don't really pay the bills, but those are the things that keep me going. People who love art are going to continue to do art regardless, but it comes down a lot of the time to "I got to pay rent." You got to do what you got to do. I made burritos for many years. [*laughter*] Last year was the first time that I tried to focus more on my art.

**Nia:** When I saw you speak at Oakland Nights Live, you showed this image of you as a butterfly and you talked about using art to combat stereotypes of how gay men are supposed to look. When did body image become part of your art and your activism? Is that something recent or something you've been thinking about for a while?

**Julio:** I think that's more recent. When I was in college, I heard about *The Panza Monologues*. It's kind of based on *The Vagina Monologues* and it's about women who are like, "Take care of yourself, but at the same time don't give a fuck what people think of your body." All those fashion designers who are gay have created this idea that if you're a woman, you have to look a certain way. I never understood why gay men are that way. I think about *Will and Grace*, about the whole "gay men are into fashion" stereotype and the idea that they're supposed to tell women how to dress. I'm not like that, so does that mean I'm not gay enough or does that mean I'm not—

**Nia:** Because you don't tell women how to dress?

**Julio:** Yeah, exactly! Again, that's the danger with trying to assimilate. You have created this perfect image, so you have to be this person that the media is telling you that you are. It's this sick cycle of trying to be so perfect that then that's what you're expected to be. I had female friends who would tell me, "Let's go shopping! Be my gay!" Like I said, I've always been a big boy. When you're in the gay clubs you are bombarded with all these images, especially in our community where it's sexualized—hypersexualized.

There's a difference between being hypersexualized and being sex-positive. It's really hard to make folks understand that there's a difference there. Being sex-positive is me accepting myself, who I am, my sexuality, and not being like, "Oh, I'm not going to fuck you because you're fat" or "I'm not fucking you because you're Black." That's not sex-positivity. That's a whole other issue, and those things exist because there's this idea of using sex as a way to be accepted. That's dangerous.

I've had conversations with my partner where he tells me that when he was younger he would be harassed by men. That was not my experience because I did not fit that stereotype. Sometimes because you don't have that attention you feel like, "Oh, why aren't I getting attention?" You get caught up in that! It's really easy. But as I'm getting older, I'm like, "Whatever." I try to stay away from that world, but I was still thinking, "I'm not that." Just because I made that image doesn't mean I'm entirely like, "I'll take off my shirt." I don't have that self-assurance. But I have art! I'm like, "Alright. This is a step for me to even take off my shirt, take a picture of myself, and use it for a drawing." It's a big step for me. I connect it to the butterfly because it's who I am. Being queer is more than my sexuality, more than my body parts…

It's the same with being undocumented: being undocumented is about more than trying to get papers. Being queer and undocumented are two of my identities that are part of who I am, but they're not *who* I am. It's important to use those identities and to be like, "Yeah, this is who I am, and I'm not the only one." I got really good feedback from other folks, especially folks who are on the chubby side, and they're like, "Oh my god, thank you for making this."

Another project I'm part of, the "Undocumented and Awkward" videos, came out of something else. My roommate is actually one of the co-founders of Dreamers Adrift and when we were in college, we started working on this project where we wanted to use media to highlight the stories of undocumented immigrants—

undocumented students, because we were students—but that project sort of fell through.

**Nia:** What was the original intention for the project?

**Julio:** The project was called "1.8 Million Dreams," based on the 1.8 million students who would potentially have benefitted from the DREAM Act. Our goal was to create a website where people could upload their stories and then to collect 1.8 million stories. That sounded like an amazing project.

But when you work with folks who are not undocumented, it's like, "Art is more important than the activism." For us, no—they go hand in hand. It was becoming about the art and not about the activism, so some personal issues arose out of that project, and it didn't work out.

The folks who were undocumented in the group—there were four of us—still wanted to do something creative, but we didn't know what. In November of 2010, when the DREAM Act was about to be voted on and everybody was hoping that it was going to happen, we just sort of put a camera in front of us. At first we were like, "What do we do? Blog videos?" We told our own stories and put ourselves out there.

One day it was just the four of us and we wanted to create an altar for Day of the Dead to represent the dreams that have passed, people who have given up on their dreams, and to represent future dreams. We had what was basically a flip camera and we filmed ourselves putting the altar together, then we put it up online. People really dug it. Like, "Oh, that's a different way of telling a story."

We started making more videos like that. We were all film buffs and liked sketch comedy. At first it was kind of serious, with sad music. Then we saw that people were using these videos to share a different idea of being undocumented. We wanted to get away from that whole thing of putting somebody in front of a camera and telling a story. Rather than doing that, we were like, "Let's act out a story." We started doing those videos and people really dug them.

Then we started talking about how a lot of us are—when we talk about being undocumented—really sad, because being undocumented can be awkward and sad and some stories are horrible. We were like, "But we need to make fun of this. We need to use humor as a way to cope with this," because that's what we do. If you see a lot of our Facebook messages to each other, it's clear that we try to be funny because we can't feel sorry for ourselves all the time.

We started talking about how telling somebody that you're undocumented can be awkward, so the title "Undocumented and Awkward" came up. Then we started getting all these ideas from other folks, like, "Oh my god, this one time it was really awkward 'cause…" The whole point of that was not just us creating videos, but also collaborating with other folks and pushing other folks to create their own media.

Media comes in so many different forms. It's important for us to create our own media because we can have control over that. We don't have control of what the mainstream media does, so I'm really happy that people really passed it on.

**Nia:** I really love the "Undocumented and Awkward" videos. I think I watched them all in one night. [*laughter*] Of course, my favorite is the one with you and Yosimar Reyes. Could you tell that story?

**Julio:** [*laughter*] That story came up after I went on a date, and I told the person I was undocumented. Turned out he was a Republican. A gay Republican. A gay Latino Republican! *God*! [*laughter*] It was so embarrassing. We had this argument and I was really embarrassed and ashamed of being undocumented because he made me feel really bad.

We started doing the "Undocumented and Awkward" videos around February 2011. We were talking, coming up with ideas. A lot of the videos look painfully awkward and real because most of the time they were based on real stories. That video was based on that experience I had. I invited Yosimar Reyes, who's hilarious, to be in the video. I think he's so funny in his poetry and the way he performs. I was like, "Yo! So we have this idea. Do you want to collab?" And he was like, "Yeah, yeah, girl. Let's do it. Let's do it."

It was really fun playing the person who made me feel really bad because it was like therapy. The messed up part was that all the fucked up shit I was saying as this character came so naturally because you hear all these things all the time. It was funny because Yosimar was like, "Girl, if you were telling me those things in real life, I would not be here more than a minute." It was funny because I told Yosimar, "Yeah, I went on a second date with him…" [*laughter*] I was young. I didn't know. But it was really cool to be able to portray that thing again. It's about having control of it. I didn't have control of what happened at the time. Looking back, I was like, "That was funny." I try to find humor in everything.

Transcribed by Gunjan Chopra

## Nick Mwaluko
*Trigger warning: reference to female genital mutilation*

**Nick Mwaluko:** In those days, when I was your young age [*laughter*] and living in Kenya, that's how we did it. In Kenya, Tanzania, Uganda, that's how we did it. We were cowards. The AIDS crisis was going on at the same time, too—

**Nia King:** That's how you did what, exactly?

**Nick:** That's how we were lesbian, gay, bisexual, trans, whatever else. There was so much fear. We took all that violence that the government was aiming at us and took it out on each other. It made us do strange things to each other and our community because of fear, anxiety, doubt, uncertainty, and the prospect of dying at the hands of the government.

Especially when you saw someone who was kind of in your category or playing your same role, it was almost like the hatred spiked, especially if that person had more liberty and freedoms than you did—and you often thought they did have more freedom than you because, at first glance, the grass is always greener on the other side. It was bad and you had to do it because if you didn't do it, the government would get you and you'd die, so you had to do it.

**Nia:** You had to do what?

**Nick:** You had to betray other queers. You had to tell other people who could then put that person in jeopardy. You had to pinpoint.

Let's say you're butch or you're masculine and you're going out with a feminine woman. She gets caught or people hear that she's with you. Now, how come you're friends? You don't go shopping together! Why are you friends? What exactly do you have in common? This is the thinking from those outside your community. People are suspicious.

They start talking. She, the feminine woman, is in her twenties, in her thirties. There's no boyfriend on the scene. This is odd. But it's *this one*—this one keeps coming. There's an influence here. They don't like it. They sit her down. Well, what's she going to say? She's going to say, "Well, that person keeps coming on to me. That person thinks, acts, believes they are masculine. I don't do that. Look at me."

Then they deal with you. Of course, your parents are like, "Well, the evidence is there. You look boyish, you're acting like a dude." You lose your job. You go penniless and fish food out of garbage cans. You're sleeping on the ground. You're confused. You're lost. You have nobody. You can't really reach out to her again—it's risky for her. And you do care about her. It's not like you don't.

All those things are happening and then you see another one who looks like you—butch. You see that they're dressed well, they can eat, they can get a job, they have a job, they can keep their job, and so you're kind of jealous. Sometimes you do things out of that jealousy. You take revenge. You take their girlfriend, maybe. [*laughter*] But you do *something* because you're like, "Well, I'm actually paying for the freedom that that other masculine person is enjoying. My body's being punished for the thing that you're enjoying, and I'm going to make you pay for that."

We did a lot of that. We did a *lot* of that, and more. I just wanted to write a play [*Waafrika*] where the person would actually have the guts—no matter what was happening to them or what was going to be done to them—to say, "You can do whatever you want. This is who I am. You can't take that away from me."

I wanted to write a character that way because I feel like the movement in Africa is a little timid. It's like we're waiting for the West to come in and help us and give us the formula. From what I see, there are two sides in the West, even in the gay communities: there's the Black gay community, or the people of color, and then there's the white gay community. It seems like when the white people are safe, then "gay life" is safe—according to the media, I mean. The media seems to portray the safety and security of white, largely gay male life as the mouthpiece and spotlight for all queer people, including those of color in the Western world. I see it very, very differently.

More importantly, within our community, we have the ancestors to deal with. For a lot of us, our parents are the reason we're free. They fought for independence, and so did our grandparents. We don't want them in exile. We don't want to say, "Fuck you." We legitimately want them in our lives, so we need to have that dialogue. I don't feel like that's part of the conversation in the West. White people's parents didn't really fight for them to be free.

I feel like, if we could create a movement where we're having conversations about the things that are important to us in our community—our way of dealing with this animal, this beast—then I feel that would be useful. I feel we must create an independent, spiritually-based liberation movement specifically for people of color, something that mirrors liberation theology of our African ancestors in America. Something similar to Gandhi's drive for Indian independence through peaceful, non-violent protest. His teachings spoke to the very core of his people and their way of managing their very unique struggle against oppression. We need something along those lines for queers of color.

What I feel is not useful is these NGOs [non-governmental organizations or nonprofits] coming in and dumping money, then using fifty percent of the budget for their flight plans for Westerners coming in, and then not paying the African activists who are actually going to the villages and rural areas and risking their lives. I understand why the African activists do it, but I don't think the Western model—that single-issue model—is *ever* going to work for people of color. That last part, I hope, stays in the podcast. [*laughter*]

**Nia:** I will not cut that out. You have my word.

**Nick:** [*laughter*]

**Nia:** My dad's best friend is from Uganda, and he teaches social work at Simmons College in Boston. He takes a group of social work students to Uganda every year and a couple years ago I went with them. They were—I think—all white women. We went to a bunch of different NGOs to see how social services are organized in Uganda, and one of the things that I saw was that a lot of the NGOs seemed to be owned and run by Westerners.

They hire other Westerners to do the jobs that it seems like they should be training Africans to do so that they can become self-sustaining, self-run organizations. It seems like they should be building skills among the folks who are already there instead of coming in with their expertise and then leaving…or not leaving.

Another thing I saw—and I don't feel like I understand this phenomenon completely—is that when Westerners come in, it displaces people. It raises the cost of living… I mean, I don't want to say it's like gentrification because—

**Nick:** But it is! It is like it, right? [*laughter*]

**Nia:** Is it?

**Nick:** There's a certain value to white skin all over the world, a certain privilege that comes with it. This is nothing against the Westerner or white skin or whatever it is—it's just a reality.

I wasn't colonized in the classic sense of the word—I mean, not the way my parents or my grandparents were—but I had to work my mind from that mental slavery of "When it looks white, it's supposed to be better than me." That's how I was raised. White people were viewed as superior not because of their money and wealth, but literally because "They will speak English better, and they will be able to do math better, and they'll be able to read better, and they'll be able to understand better. And anything that looks like you probably can't do it as well."

With that comes a certain kind of "We know you're not supposed to be living here, but we'll do the best that we can to make it as civilized as possible. We will do everything in our little, poverty-ridden African power to cater to your privilege in our little, unimportant village and tiny, underdeveloped communities." That way of thinking is very much there in rural Africa. We've been successfully colonized, mentally.

We don't take trips to South Africa to see the reality. We didn't do it then, and we don't now. In Tanzania, we don't take trips to Uganda, we don't take trips to Kenya. West Africa's a bit different—they travel a little bit. But we don't.

I think the best thing sometimes that can happen to you is that you're falling, you're falling, you're falling, and you have no one who'll catch you. You think you *will* die, then you realize, "No, I have this inner strength, this deep resilience, and it's there, and I've never used it. Why? Because I never had to." I feel like that's what we need. We don't need outside forces, which really don't have our best interests at heart, coming in, telling us how to live, and pitying us and thinking that their way of living is the only way to live because it's a more "civilized" standard. I think if we can do it for ourselves, we can adopt the kind of posture needed before people who are supposed to be "better than us." I'm not saying they're less than, but I don't see anything *better than* us.

Nigeria is doing it. You can see Nigerians are interested in education. They're interested in all these other things, and they're saying, "Nigeria for Nigerians." Nothing wrong with that, I don't think. I don't think it's jingoistic. I don't think it's nationalistic. I mean, Lord knows that to break into the American theater, I'd have to change my name to "Smith"! [*laughter*] I would! Otherwise, I'm not really an American, no matter how long I stay here. But if someone from the Western world comes to Africa with a play, they go straight to the National Theatre because they must be great writers proficient in their language! Which may or may not lead to strong storytelling, but that's not the point, is it?

This is the truth. I think it was before 2000 that for me to get the visa to come here, I could not be HIV-positive. If I were HIV-positive, I would be banned from travel. But the opposite was not true: for an American to get a visa to go to Tanzania, Kenya, or Uganda, it didn't matter whether they were HIV-positive or not. So then, what are you saying about my life? What are you saying about *our* lives? If our governments are undermining our own value—our own lives—then what do the others who are outside looking in think of us?

I think we *need* that backbone, and if it means certain generations are crushed…it has to be that way.

I'm being a realist. Julius Nyerere, the first president of Tanzania, died not seeing the beauty of the Tanzania that he had designed. The state of Tanzania that existed when he was on his deathbed was a far cry from the vision he yearned to create at the inception of independence. Since his death, we have inched closer and closer to his vision: we've never had a civil war, we've never been plagued by tribalism, and we've never had a coup d'état. Never. I'm not saying it's peaceful, but I don't look at a Tanzanian and say, "What tribe are you?" because of all of Nyerere's efforts to make it *one* Tanzania. He died not seeing this, but it was a great vision. Mao died not seeing the greatness that China's becoming. All I'm saying is, invest in the citizens who make up your country, rather than outsiders who do not have your best interest at heart.

We keep giving away our pain to the West, and we know historically what Westerners do with Black people's pain: they enslave it and they make money off of it and they kick it and they make it bleed and then they go back and say how great they are because of all the money they've made from milking Black people's pain. White people worship Black people's pain at a distance because they want genuine pain without the suffering and struggle that are pain's twins. "Westerner" is a euphemism for "white." I'm not a racist. I'm really not. I'm just looking at it and saying, "Well, when will I be a human being? Why must I have your permission to be fully human?"

**Nia:** You said that to break into the American theater scene you'd have to change your name to "Smith." How *did* you break in? How did you become interested in playwriting, and then how did you get your play *Waafrika* produced?

**Nick:** I wrote a lot of fiction and would submit it everywhere. Everything came bouncing back—rejection, rejection. Then I wrote a lot of poetry and I wrote a lot of other things. I think it was because of school. I was failing the fiction class because you have to get all those books and that was expensive, so I said, "Well, what can I do that's only pen and paper?" and they said, "Try playwriting."

I went in and wrote a scene. It was a very bad scene. The person who read the scene turned the paper over so my words were facedown against the tabletop. The back of the paper was facing up towards the ceiling. It got me very, very upset. At night, I just said to myself, "Well, Nick, have you ever gotten that upset over anything else you've written?" and I said, "No, never, not over any other writing I've done." If so much emotion was generated, I felt there must be a reason why. I reasoned it was because I cared about writing plays.

**Nia:** Why did they turn the paper over?

**Nick:** It was a really bad scene. It was such a bad scene. It was just like, nobody talks that way. [*laughter*] Like, "What is this scene about?"

**Nia:** So not bad as in violent, like "I can't read this," but bad like "This is not well-written."

**Nick:** "This is not well-written." Nobody talks like this. There's nobody who's like this. I'd violated almost all the basic principles that make up the foundation of playwriting in a single scene, and it showed! She was a good actress and a great reader, so when she turned it over, it got me upset. I thought, "Well, maybe if there's so much emotion over this, maybe this is the thing."

I came in with another scene after listening to other people's feedback and something clicked. I liked doing it. Then later on I thought, "Well, why not submit?" I kept submitting—I've been rejected quite a bit—but then I had a play of mine published. The woman who's doing the play now, Nicole Stodard, she read the play and wrote a critique online, so I emailed her and thanked her. She asked, "Can I produce that play?" and I said, "Sure." Then we just kept in touch.

**Nia:** How did the woman who ended up producing your play find it?

**Nick:** It was published. She read it and wrote a critique of it without ever reaching out to me at all, so I found her critique online, read it, and reached out to her to thank her.

**Nia:** So you just found her critique of your play on the Internet?

**Nick:** Yeah! I was like, "What the…?!" I said to her, "Thanks a lot for doing this" and we kept in touch. She told me a little bit about herself and why she's interested, and I liked talking to her. The thing is, she kept saying, "Nick, I want this to be pure—my experience in the theater." I quite appreciated that. Her sister had died of cancer. Once her sister died—quite young—she wanted to commit herself fully to making theater. I thought, "I want to be with this person because the calling is coming from a special place." I like Nicole, I like working with her. We're friends.

**Nia:** How are you feeling about the reviews that are coming back? It seems like they're mixed reviews. [*laughter*]

**Nick:** Right?

**Nia:** It seems like people are really spellbound by the final scene. That's something that has been written about a lot. I read a couple of the reviews that you sent me and there seem to be themes. People agree that the last scene is totally mind-blowing…and horrific. People seem to agree that you write the language for the African characters really beautifully, and the critics also seem to think that the language of the white characters is a lot more stilted. How do you feel about the feedback that you're getting?

**Nick:** I'm glad that they came out to see and review the play and everything, but I feel like, what do they know about how Africans talk?

I think Bobby, the white character, is a very real character and her language is real. One of the criticisms—not from the reviewers, but from some people—has been that she has no flaws, that she's too perfect. I think it's almost the opposite: she's too selfish, she's too one-sided, she's too single-minded in her drive, purpose, and motivations. At the same time, Bobby keeps the dream alive. She keeps telling Awino, "You can do this thing." She sustains their relationship for much of the play. Awino is always unstable, forever uncertain—"Go, leave, go, leave, stay, go, leave." Bobby's like, "I will do what you say, but you can do this thing." To me, that's one of Bobby's quintessential virtues.

In one of the reviews, it says, "From a sociological point of view, this is probably the most important thing you'll see in the theater this year," but the sociological aspects that they list are all the African things. I also think that maybe white people should look at themselves because right now, with *Beasts of the Southern Wild* and a couple things—they're writing our stories, frankly. They're writing, in *Beasts of the Southern Wild*, how a Black man deals with his daughter.

I have questions about that, about the tenderness that is lacking. You want to make that stereotypical Strong Black Woman, and you think these are the scenes—but, whatever. Fine. So you're doing it. You got some roles, you got some actors. But Tarantino's thing of giving the gun to the bandit...what was that movie called?

**Nia:** *Django Unchained*?

**Nick:** *Django*. If I were a runaway slave roaming the woods and a white man came along to give me a gun, who would be the first person I'd shoot?! [*laughter*] So that's it. That story's over in the first fucking minute.

But alright. You got your awards, you got your acclaim, you got your great actors. But I want you to know how I see you, as a lesbian, as an African, as a trans person, as a writer, as a playwright, as a citizen, as a political entity, as a lover, as a hater. As someone with an array of complex, meaningful, unscripted experiences with white people in and outside of the queer community, I want to communicate to you how I see you.

I have a unique lens that informs how I have to navigate who you are when you enter into my world. I'm not going to change it. As a writer, I refuse to change it because I think people need to hear and see it, especially white people. I mean, you do *Lion King*, you tell me how you see Africa, and I have to sit there and clap. I want you to know I see you like this, and I don't think Bobby is a particularly spiteful character.

Bobby is the kind of white person I *wish* I could have in my corner. In the conditional tense—I *wish*. I wish I could have somebody that fierce. I wish I could have somebody willing to die for me. That's not just white or Black. It happens to be that she's white. Making her white was simply because, with a white woman, you *know* people are going to look on the street in a rural village because she's the only white one living in a rural village. It's easier to say these are the Western dreams. If I had an African American character—a Black character—I don't know if I would be that comfortable writing the play the way I did because, in a sense, Bobby is persecuted by the community. Do I want to persecute an African American character, as the writer?

Another person might write that story, but that's not a story that I want to tell. It would be harder for me to write because I feel like African Americans *are* African, they *do* belong in the community, and they wouldn't go to the burial ground without understanding what it means to a group of Africans. I just feel like they would know the sacred, celebrated place of the church at the burial ground, but *Bobby* would go there because of the way Bobby is. I just feel like she is not as spiritual. I don't know—maybe these are all stereotypes, prejudices. Maybe my ear is not attuned to white characters, but this is what I see when I see them. This is how I see them because I've been loved and fucked and fucked over by them.

Reviewers have compared my play *Waafrika* to *Ruined*. Lynn Nottage won the Pulitzer Prize for *Ruined*. She had a whole team working on that play with her. I mean, it's just me and Nicole working day and night, you know?

**Nia:** You said that maybe you're not attuned to writing white characters. My question is whether or not you think Western audiences are attuned to *you*. I haven't seen the play, but some of the things that you're representing, like female genital mutilation [FGM], are such incredibly loaded issues. There's already sort of a way of talking about FGM in the West that doesn't seem to be informed much at all by African opinions or experiences. I think that makes it hard, as a person who is critical of Western imperialism and its relationship to Western feminism, to know where to stand. I mean…no amount of moral relativism makes female genital mutilation look good.

I always worry, when I try to represent communities of color in my work, about how other people are going to look at it, whether those people are white or they're other people of color who are going to say, "We don't want to be represented this way. We don't want our dirty laundry out there. This isn't the kind of stuff we want people thinking about us." Do you feel like the audiences in South Florida that are going to see this play about Africa have any way to understand the nuance and complexity—or even just the broad strokes—of this play and what you're trying to do with it?

**Nick:** I think the access, hopefully, is through the emotion. I think we all know what it's like to live a lie that is killing us. I think we all know what it's like not to claim the person we love. I feel like we all know what it's like to flaunt an identity without actually claiming that identity, and it's kind of hidden and tucked inside for a safer space on a safer day that never quite arrives. I think we all know that we're fully alive when we claim something that's so sacred to us because it is our essential core.

I don't feel like it's my responsibility to make people comfortable with the way in which death is almost an everyday thing. When I was a kid, I had two brothers who died. People die *all* the time. It's a big deal, yes, but it's also not a big deal because a lot of people die because of typhoid, malaria, AIDS, whatever. They die because they don't have enough money to buy Malaraquin at the kiosk. They die because we all will die.

In East Africa, the Luo tribe puts the dead body out for thirty days. You have to touch it. Whether you're a child or not, you see it rotting. It's out there in the open. This is their tribal custom. Nobody is shielded from the inevitable reality of death, no matter how lofty your title or how distinguished your place in your tribal community. It seems to me white Americans try to shield themselves from the inevitability of death—they refuse to age, refuse to accept their bodies' natural maturation. All that stuff seems a bit silly to me.

I don't know, because I haven't been to see the play in Florida, but from what Nicole tells me, the audience cries. They laugh. They're there. Even though the chief has many wives, they know that that session with the wives sitting together talking about things is women's talk. I feel that maybe the audience can understand it.

The critics or the reviewers *say* they want a new voice, and they *say* they want new stories, and they *say* they want these things, but I don't know if they're actually committed to it. Some of the writers create work in which the white person is always a threat, and the African characters have very little power over Mighty Whitey. My question always is, past 1960 or 1950, why would I have such a white person in my life? I just wouldn't write that person because blood has already been shed, people have already done the work so that I can be free, so why would I go back to that slavery? I wouldn't have them in my life, let alone fuck them or let them fuck me. [*laughter*] To me it's like, well, Bobby may get it wrong, and critics may not *want* to see that white person—by which I mean a white person in service of a Black person—but that's who I would still write given the choice.

What the critics don't see is that Bobby stays. What they don't see is that Bobby is committed to the "nth" degree. What they don't see is that she's the custodian of the dream for a long part of the play. What they don't see is that Bobby's hatred of white people means that she can never really have Awino love her because she's alienated from herself, too. What the critics don't see or refuse to acknowledge is the idea that there can be and are white allies committed to an ideal while blind to all the avenues their privilege affords them. What they don't see is where they refuse to go, though the play takes them there. So they don't see all those things, they don't want to bring them in. And from a sociological point of view, I feel like that's *just* as important, but it's never mentioned because they're so fixated on "There's no white person on the earth like this." Oh, yes, there are. It's just maybe they're not your friends. [*laughter*]

The other part of it is the critics are like, "The sex comes in and it's just too mind-boggling." It's a graphic sex scene. I was just like, "Well, maybe the critics need to be fucked by a lesbian to know how graphic it can be! And how good it can be!" [*laughter*] I mean, you're just free! You know what I'm saying? If the government is going to kill you for fucking, you *fuck*. Keep that in the podcast. [*laughter*]

**Nia:** I will not take that out. Why would I take that out? [*laughter*]

**Nick:** You fuck to the "nth" degree because the gun is right there at your temple and between your legs. I mean, we *fucked*. We really fucked. We *had* to fuck because it was your last fuck every time!

This should be in the Bible: "When you fuck and it's your last fuck, you *fuck*." Let me tell you: you fuck, you suck, you lick, you do it all because, shit! You don't *know* when it's going to come to an end! I was like, "Well, clearly the critics hadn't had sex in a while." [*laughter*]

It was crazy. I mean, we did it outside. I was helped by the fact that I looked like a boy. They would always be like, [*whispers*] "We're going to get caught. We're going to get caught." I'd be like, "No, we won't." Nobody would suspect that we would actually have the guts to do it. But it was *good*! Because of course there's the attraction and all that, but part of the beauty was that you knew this could be your last time, so you *gave* your last. You gave it all. Oh my god. To me, sex at the time was synonymous with love. It really was, because I was giving my last *all* the time. It was great training. It was like the Olympics of fucking. [*laughter*]

I don't really care what the critics say. I care a lot about what an audience goes away with, and what Nicole says. Not that the play is parallel at all to it, but *The Color Purple* by Alice Walker, and the transition that the men in the book went through—people gave her a lot of heat for that. But in that novel, the principal relationships are female relationships and we saw such a range. We saw such a range and it was so beautiful to see. In a patriarchal society, watching those women, and what women could be when men are at the center of the world—women who have been disenfranchised, damaged, and hurt for centuries. I mean, it was beautiful, and so if it came at the cost of all that noise…

The reason for writing the play was to help my personal fears and how I'm easily overwhelmed, but it really was also to say, "You guys, we don't need to hide, and we don't need to hurt each other like this. We can have this conversation and survive it, and if we don't survive it, the fact that we've died and we've left something so sacred for the next generation to work with justifies a life spent in pursuit of certain vanities like safety and security. This was an important thing—for *us*."

Transcribed by Gunjan Chopra

**Leah Lakshmi Piepzna-Samarasinha**
*This interview was conducted by email.*

**Nia King:** How do you identify?

**Leah Lakshmi Piepzna-Samarasinha:** I am a queer, disabled, cis, mixed-race (Sri Lankan/Irish/Ukrainian) femme writer, performer, healer, and teacher.

**Nia:** What do you do for a living?

**Leah:** I see being a writer, performer, teacher, and educator as my primary job. This didn't come easy or overnight. In 2006, I quit the nonprofit day job I had as a tenant hotline counselor after a gradual process of building up experience and a little bit of savings and learning from other self-employed artists without trust funds about how they do it. Currently (2014), I teach writing classes in Oakland and online, focused on creating writing spaces for queer, trans, and Two-Spirit, Black, Indigenous, and People of Color writers and 2QTPOC [Two-Spirit, queer, and trans people of color] with disabilities and chronic illnesses. I do a lot of college gigs, performing and teaching writing, disability justice, and transformative justice workshops.

Sometimes, I get paid to write or perform, like with Sins Invalid. I co-direct Mangos With Chili, a queer and trans people of color arts collective, with my friend and comrade Cherry Galette. I have a tarot business—Brownstargirl Tarot—that is a chunk of change. For the past five years, I've also taught sexual health exam techniques (e.g. how to do pelvic and breast exams from a trans-competent, trauma-aware, and comfortable perspective) to medical and nurse practitioner students and health professionals through Project Prepare, a feminist health organization—occasional work that pays well. A million hustles, but I like being self-employed.

**Nia:** Do you see yourself as an artist?

**Leah:** Oh, yes. I write poetry, memoir/creative nonfiction, journalistic articles sometimes, and zines. I also edit books and create talks. I also like creating performance that fuses movement, ritual, and storytelling. I like thinking of the stage as a sacred moment in time that oppressed people can control even when we can't control so much, where we can create a world that is hyper-real, that is a portal to another reality where ancestors visit, where dreams can walk with us, where we can tell secrets and imagine what's possible.

**Nia:** Do you consider your work to be political?

**Leah:** Oh, yes. What June Jordan said really resonates with me: "To tell the truth is to become beautiful, to begin to love yourself, value yourself. And that's political, in its most profound way." She also said, "You cannot write lies and write good poetry."

I work with issues of race, class, disability, gender, sexuality, and survivorhood. I think telling the truth about those stories is, as Chrystos said, "powerful medicine" that is deeply needed and inherently political in a white capitalist colonialist ableist patriarchy, where corporate media and art-making is rooted in universal deceit. Growing up, I had that experience of feeling like I was "crazy." The ways I saw reality and experienced it weren't reflected in any media I saw. Finding feminist and queer-of-color writing changed that and for real saved my life.

**Nia:** Do you feel that higher education has helped you in your career as an artist?

**Leah:** Sort of. It's a complicated question to answer. My mother stressed education and pushed me really hard to get straight 'A's, look good on applications, and get into a legit, four-year university. She had had limited access to higher education and came from a family where education was not valued for her as a girl. It was very clear to her that education was an incredible privilege and a "ticket out." My father also does not have a university degree and this, combined with racism he faces as an immigrant, South Asian man, impacted his ability to find and keep work.

I applied to, I don't know, fourteen or seventeen schools and my mother said, "Awesome, you're going to go wherever gives you the most financial aid." That ended up being New York University in 1993. Being in New York in the mid-nineties on my own was a much bigger huge amazing catalyst of everything about being a writer and performer than school itself ever was. School was pretty boring. I'd read most of the books already, there were a lot of white rich kids from Long Island in huge classes, and it was easy to get 'A's. But I met Nicole Demarin—a white, working-class, survivor, queer feminist visual artist—when I was hung over doing clinic defense against Operation Rescue at an abortion clinic at 6AM. She took me home, fed me, and mentored me for a year.

I was her "intern," working with her and her friends who were putting together a feminist art show called "No More Nice Girls" at ABC NO RIO—a punk, squatted arts space on the Lower East Side. She did this all from her living room while eating takeout and smoking Newports. It was from her that I learned how to write a call for submissions, look at artwork, curate a show, do promo, and figure out money. She gave me this whole vision of being a working-class, feminist, femme, queer artist. She worked as a secretary at Hunter College during the day, and all the art she and her friends did they did on their own time and out-of-pocket, which included incredible installations about HIV/AIDS. They'd wheatpaste posters in bodegas and on the street memorializing the dead.

Soaking up student-of-color, young feminist, and queer-of-color organizing, going to poetry performances at the Nuyorican Poets Café, Brooklyn Moon, and other poetry spots, and reading books standing up in bookstores that stayed open late was my education. But when I had friends who hadn't gone to school or who had dropped out, I resisted that—they were mostly more class-privileged folks who had more of a safety net in a way that I didn't. Or they were my cousins and friends who were working-class white and POC kids who were stuck in Worcester, Massachusetts, working shitty jobs.

I always carried with me how hard my mom had had to fight to go to school, how she got a teaching degree from Worcester State College—which is a really broke-ass small college in Worcester—by a fluke. She was working in the office of a local shoe factory after graduation and somehow her former English teacher saw her and said, "I'm going to try and connect you with a school." She got in late and went against total family disapproval. This is an amazing story and it's also a story of how her white privilege and class non-privilege both were at play. I knew how important that piece of paper [a diploma] was, and all the students of color and/or working-class and poor students I knew at NYU felt the same way.

After I graduated, I didn't go on to grad school like a lot of folks I was in school with did. I left the US and moved to Toronto, where I was involved in writing, performing, activism, and just survival for a long time. I was working on a prison justice newspaper, working as an abortion counselor, doing organizing with other psychiatric survivors, cleaning houses, telemarketing, landscaping, and just doing a lot of writing, reading, healing, and living. I was also really, really sick with CFIDS [Chronic Fatigue and Immune Dysfunction Syndrome] and fibromyalgia and was hit really deeply with dealing with being an incest survivor. Those were really tough years financially and in many other ways. However, I have never regretted the decision to move to Toronto and not go on to graduate school right away.

I left New York for a lot of reasons: one of them was that I thought most of academia was bullshit and it was killing me. I felt really blocked from being able to write in the classes I had been in because there were no ground rules, no grounding in the reasons why it is hard for marginalized writers to tell our stories. It took me a few years to feel like I had gotten my voice back, like I could write and speak. In Toronto, there was and is an incredible creative community by and for QTPOC. In the nineties, Sister Vision Women of Color Press and the writers it nurtured were a real presence in the city. Desh Pardesh, a radical, South Asian diasporic festival that was queer and feminist and anti-classist, was incredibly important to me and was one of the first places I ever performed. And there was also a huge dub poetry community, huge numbers of Indigenous writers producing work, performing, and publishing. I learned a lot from listening to and reading these writers.

In 2005 and 2006, I went to VONA's [Voices of Our Nation Arts Foundation's] amazing writing retreat for writers of color, which changed my life and showed me what politicized arts education could be. That experience pushed me to create community-based writing programs like Toronto's Asian Arts Freedom School, which I co-founded with Gein Wong in 2005, and Pink Ink, a writing program for queer, trans, and Two Spirit youth. Those spaces were and are incredibly important to me and were spaces that felt so much more important than any traditional, white-dominated academic space.

The idea of graduate school kept poking at me, though. Going was a really hard decision, but I finally said yes, got into Mills College, and moved back to Oakland and the US for the first time in a decade in 2007. I did it partly because I had been away from the US for ten years and I wanted to go back. I also wanted to maybe be able to teach writing someday. I was also really, really scared to apply and go to graduate school. I was afraid that it would take me out of the amazing community of QTPOC writers I was in, into some bullshit where I would be surrounded by white girls named Emily, and where I'd owe a lot of money for some bullshit. Leaving for graduate school meant leaving the community, safety net, and access strategies I had built up. When I visited Mills, Justin Chin, who was teaching the class I sat in on, said to me, "Why do you want to go here? You're going to be really annoyed." I said, "I know, but I want to have your job someday, maybe?" He just nodded.

Now, when folks ask me about that graduate school experience, I always say that it made me tighten up my game kind of despite itself. A lot of college was bullshit, but even with that, it forced me to take myself more seriously and fight to win with my work. I did learn a ton about teaching from studying with June Jordan's Poetry for the People program at UC Berkeley while I was going to Mills. That program was the single best thing about my graduate school experience—a program rooted in Black feminist liberation writing pedagogy where we got to learn and practice teaching writing and performance poetry.

At the end of the day, that piece of paper does give you privilege, open doors, and allow for more opportunities than someone who doesn't have it. I'm glad I can teach at the college level if I want to because I have an MFA, but I am also committed to the community-based arts practices I am part of. I always want to tell people that you don't have to go through formal education as your only route to art.

**Nia:** Where do you consider yourself to be in your career?

**Leah:** I guess early mid-career? Three books, one big award, and a couple more books on the way. I'm thirty-eight—that's mid-career, right? It's not like Margaret Atwood's mid-career, though. I don't know. It's interesting, being my age, a queer disabled cis writer of color, and looking at where I am now. It's interesting to see, out of who you worked with, who's still doing stuff and who's not. Things have changed so much, especially in POC and QPOC performance and spoken word. It kind of floors me to think about performers who were famous and blowing up five or six years ago, who some younger QTPOC have barely heard of now.

Spoken word has changed so much since the mid-nineties. I can remember in the nineties when it was totally underground and no one was expecting to get paid, ever. Then there was the Def Poetry Jam era in the early-2000s where some folks were making a ton of money, to now, the Recession era. I feel like it's come full circle in some ways. Pepsi is not giving anyone five thousand dollars to write a "slam poem" for an ad anymore.

I am grateful for the success I've had, but I'm still pretty broke. I'm chronically ill, so working a nine-to-five job is not an option—I get sick too often. I'm not part of the literary establishment and I don't have a ton of security. There are gifts that come with being an artist who writes and performs for your community, and I've always written and performed thinking of it as a service and gift to my community. The hard part is what happens if your community moves, dies, forgets about you, or disagrees with you?

**Nia:** Where do you want to go from here?
**Leah:** I want to write more books, teach writing in community-based and college settings, save up to buy a house, have a kid. I am dreaming of creating a rural writing retreat space by and for

QTPOC that is crip-centered[3] and accessible. I want to continue to build and be part of a beloved community.

**Nia:** Do you worry that you may face identity-based challenges in getting to where you want to go?

**Leah:** Um, fuck yeah. It's bizarre: there's this huge, vibrant, fractious, amazing world of queer and trans, feminist-of-color, disabled art- and culture-making that is so huge when you're in it, and then when you step outside of it you realize that there are all these other worlds that have no idea who we are or that we exist.

I've been trying to get a memoir published for a while. Publishing has been super impacted by the Recession and it has also *always* been bullshit for QTPOC. I still get "Wow, it sounds like there's a limited market for that"—"that" being a memoir by a queer, POC, cis, disabled survivor, even though there are five million kinda blah white middle-class girl memoirs on the bookstore remainder shelf. It's frustrating.

**Nia:** Do you feel supported as an artist here in the Bay Area?

**Leah:** Yes and no. This place can be like Candyland for QTPOC crip artists—there's so much shit happening all the time! It's really inspiring, I've learned a lot, and I don't want to take it for granted. At the same time, there was a sense of possibility when I moved here in 2007, of living room, that I feel has diminished. Maybe I just need a break, but the Recession coupled with all the Google and gentrifier bullshit has raised rents, tightened the housing

---

3 "Crip" is a word that has been reclaimed by some in the disability community. It used to be primarily used pejoratively and, like "queer," is still used pejoratively by some.

market, and contributes to this sense that people are fighting over the crumbs. Desperation makes hope and possibility hard.

Also, this is a super transient place and I've been hating that aspect of the Bay for at least the last three years. People come, people leave. There's often deep division between folks who are transplants here and folks who are from here. It makes building deep community and long-term projects harder, at least for me. I also feel like it contributes to a culture of disposability at times. I don't know—I'm a Taurus and my other home, Toronto, is a place where no one leaves, ever, so maybe I'm just missing that. But I also think the Bay can be a place where QTPOC artists dream and do big things, and I don't ever want to forget that magic or take it for granted.

**Janet Mock**
*This interview was conducted via Skype.*

**Janet Mock:** The purpose of me coming out [in *Marie Claire*] was first to stand in my truth, but also to stop telling other people's stories and start to tell my own. As a journalist, you can hide behind other people's stories, and so that's what I did. It was fulfilling when I was, like, twenty-three—in New York City—to twenty-five. Then twenty-five, twenty-six happened. I was like, "This is kind of getting repetitive and boring."

After a while I felt unfulfilled, so I started taking a memoir-writing class at New York University. I was kind of telling—writing—stories about my life. I was fictionalizing them sometimes. I was using my writing muscle to write *personal* stuff. I was kind of always third-person writing before, and I was going into first-person, and it felt so personal. Then the opportunity to tell my story to *Marie Claire* came up and my life kind of changed after that. The purpose of me opening up in such a public way—beyond just standing in my truth and giving young women like myself a story of a thriving young woman who is trans and of color, giving them a mirror—was also to be able to write and publish my own book.

When I signed my contract with Atria Books at Simon and Schuster [for *Redefining Realness: My Path to Womanhood, Identity, Love & So Much More*], they gave me a nice little advance, so I could leave my job at *People*. I do speaking here and there—that also helped pay some rent, and that enabled me to do my writing full-time and my storytelling full-time.

**Nia King:** How did you get the opportunity to tell your story in *Marie Claire*? It sounds like you didn't pitch to them—they came to you?

**Janet:** Yes. I had opened up to my friend, who I interned with at *InStyle Magazine*, about being trans, and then she told someone else. That someone else happened to be a journalist—we're all Black girls in media. It's a very small world. The journalist was someone this friend was close with—it wasn't just some random person. The woman who ended up pitching the piece to *Marie Claire* approached me after getting the okay from my friend, saying, "I've heard so much about you from our mutual friends. Would you be interested in having a conversation about what this piece could look like?"

I was at a point where I was ready to come out—I just didn't know what the opportunity was going to look like. I always thought that I would come out with the release of my book. I always thought that I would do it on my own terms. Then, the *Marie Claire* thing came along. It was pitched as a profile, so it was supposed to be written in third-person, and it ended up being written in first-person, in *my* voice, but someone else wrote it. It was this weird thing for me. As a writer, I felt like my voice was taken away.

**Nia:** How did you feel about that?

**Janet:** We were so far along in the process already. The piece was for the June 2011 issue. We had been talking about the piece since September of 2010. By the time the *Marie Claire* editors made that point-of-view switch to saying, "We want it to be in first-person," I couldn't then say, "*I'm* going to write it." This other woman pitched it, so I couldn't say that I was going to write it, even though it was a collaborative process. When the editors of *Marie Claire* said that they wanted it to be a first-person piece, the writer was like, "Do you want me to go to another magazine?" I was just like, "Let's just get this done." I was already so ready to be out.

Because I worked as an online editor for People.com, for *People Magazine*, I was equipped with all these tools already to communicate with audiences and to make language very accessible and to tell stories. When the *Marie Claire* thing came along, I was ready for that moment. My website was up. It's all about being prepared for the moment. It's not enough just to tell your story. How do you engage with people? How do you find people who want to continue engaging with you beyond this story? How do you engage with them and what do you want to do? For me, it was to continue telling stories, to write when necessary.

**Nia:** It sounds like you knew you wanted to write *Redefining Realness* since way before the *Marie Claire* piece came out.

**Janet:** Oh, yeah. The book was mentioned in the piece towards the end and that was on purpose. I was like, "We're going to do this. You need to say that I'm working on a memoir. That needs to be in there." Because I said that I was working on a memoir, people who were within the publishing industry and who read the *Marie Claire* piece approached me and said, "We hear you're working on a book. Do you need representation?" I said, "Of course!"

I had a proposal and sample chapters ready for my book. I found the representation I felt comfortable with. My agent suggested a few publishers he felt would handle my story in the right way. We met with them, had a series of meetings, and as this was going on, my profile was also changing publicly. We found a great home for the book with Atria Books at Simon and Schuster. I think I got my book deal in April, in May it was announced, and then in July I left my job.

**Nia:** You seem to have a very positive presence on social media, which is something I really admire. I think it's really hard to continually present yourself as positive and professional when people are always coming at you with negativity on Twitter, just because they can. I'm curious how you've been able to maintain such a positive presence online.

**Janet:** That's been a conscious decision. It's intentional. For me, I feel like there's enough sadness in our world—like so much calling out online—that I refuse to engage in that stuff. I also don't come from that hurt place. If something hurts me, I don't use Twitter as the outlet for it. I use my boyfriend as the outlet for it. I use my best friend as the outlet for it. I use my girlfriends as the outlet for it. I don't use social media for that. [*laughter*]

I try to find the silver lining in things. I just think that we're so steeped in trauma that I don't feel like putting more out there. I feel like people's lived experiences are already a lot to deal with, and for me to then come out and feed into that would just be adding more negativity to folks' lives.

Bad shit's happening to everyone, to a lot of people, and I'd rather use that in my writing, to talk about that and unpack it a bit, but not necessarily in a one-hundred-and-forty-character tweet, you know?

I feel like we should rally around a traumatic experience. Like, how can we rally around it and transform it? Is someone taking action? How can we then signal-boost the work of someone who's taking action around a sad circumstance, not just say, "Someone died today"? If I'm going to do a call-out, I'm going to call out a media organization, not a person.

I'm just not invested in call-out culture. I don't think it's that helpful, I don't think it's that healthy. I don't think we've come to a place as a community where we can celebrate our happiness, and the happy things that have happened in our community, so I don't want to further fall into that whole pattern of negativity, you know?

**Nia:** Yeah.

**Janet:** I think it's also that people see me as a role model. I never say that I'm a role model, but someone may see me as one, so I want to make sure that my values and ethics align across all of my platforms, whether it's Twitter, Tumblr, Facebook, or my blog. At the same time, parents of trans kids will read my blog and say that they can't let their kids read it because I write about some traumatic events and they don't want their kids to see that. To certain people, a lot of things that I'm writing about—like class, race, sex work, all of these kinds of violence, abuse, exile, and criminalization—those are scary things that people don't want to see. But it matters who's seeing that, right?

**Nia:** Yeah. That's really interesting because, first of all, that's very different from what we were talking about with call-out culture and the culture of talking trash on the Internet…

**Janet:** [*laughter*]

**Nia:** You shouldn't have to present a Disney-fied version of what it's like to walk through the world as a trans woman of color to make people feel better, even though you don't want to scare them, necessarily. Do you find yourself self-censoring for certain audiences, out of concern for how either parents of trans folks, on one hand, or just random Internet haters, on the other hand, are going to read your writing?

**Janet:** Never in my writing. Maybe slightly in my tweets. I'll think about whether or not something feels right within me, then I'll sit on the tweet for a little bit and be like, "What's the best way to craft this? What's a great way to craft this in a way that no one has before?" That's always my perspective. If everyone is being negative on something, it may mean that my voice isn't necessarily needed in that conversation. Or maybe it is needed. "How can I redirect these conversations?" That's what I'm always asking myself.

Anytime a trans woman of color is doing something, I try to boost it because I know that fewer eyes will be on it. Some people tend to expect those kinds of signal boosts from me and so it's also like, "How can I excite my audience about this? How can I make it seem new to them, that this is unique, something that they should support?" But I don't feel like I need to edit what I say. I have been trying to be more holistic about my tweets [*laughter*] because I feel like for a while right when I came out, I was tweeting trans stuff twenty-four hours a day, and then after a while I was like, "This is burning me out. I need to write about *The Real Housewives*, I need to write about *Scandal*"—tweeting about these things that are actually also part of my life.

I use Tumblr, I retweet GIFs of Beyoncé—because I'm obsessed—just kind of being more holistic about what my life looks like. Pop culture has such a huge presence within my book because it has been such a big part of my coming-of-age, how I learned who I was. Seeing Clair Huxtable in reruns of *The Cosby Show*, that's what I wanted—I wanted to be a bawse like her. [*laughter*] I wanted to be didactic and fab and all that stuff. I've been trying to incorporate that more. If something in pop culture strikes me, then I try to share it.

**Nia:** Did you always want to write about pop culture? I know you said it's always been important in your life, but I've also heard that sometimes women journalists get kind of pushed into doing what might be considered "fluffier" types of stories.

**Janet:** It's kind of where I landed. At first, I thought I was going to be a features editor at a fashion magazine. That was what I was gunning for, being at a print magazine. I never thought I was going to work online. The People.com job felt like slumming initially. The Internet was not what it is now. When I started working at People.com in 2006, there was not yet widespread use of Facebook. I think people were still kind of on MySpace—it was different. To have gotten a master's degree in journalism and to be working at a website did not feel like a dream come true at the time. I was happy I had a job working at one of the biggest brands in the world, but at the same time I was like, "I'm working for a *website*." It's not like what it is now. Now everyone's like, "Wow, you worked at People.com!"

At *People,* I didn't get to do the writing that I wanted to do, like the long-form pieces that I had been trained to do, like Joan Didion kind of writing. It was weird to be writing blurb-y things that were snappy and catchy and would make people click, but it turned out to be beneficial for all I do now. Because of working for People.com, my language as a writer is sharp and I've developed a style of writing that makes people click, that grabs people's attention.

I bring that to promoting social justice pieces. Everyone's like, "Wow, the way that you can really succinctly talk about what my piece meant in a short tweet is amazing." I'm like, "Well, that's what I did for my job." It was a lot of copyediting and that kind of craft, which is hard, coming up with headlines and titles and slugs and decks.

**Nia:** You once wrote that you never wanted to become a "poster child for the transsexual community." Do you feel like you have become a poster child, and have your feelings about that shifted at all?

**Janet:** In the author's note of my book, I say, "This is not written with the intent of representation." That was a disclaimer for me. I was saying that I'm not here to be a representative for anyone but myself and my story and my experiences.

The first criticism people love to bring up is "Oh, she's not representative of this and this and this." I was like, "Well, yeah, I said that." That's the first form of criticism—"Oh, she's passable. She's not the right kind of trans person to represent our community." No one out here can represent our whole community, but because there are so few of us visible in media, everything we say is taken as representative.

A lot of the time, I'm the first trans person that a lot of Americans will meet, because they'll see me on TV, they'll see me on *HuffPost Live*, they'll read my book, and it will be the first representation that they'll have, because maybe trans people are not out or visible in the spaces that they live in, in their everyday. Even though I give a disclaimer, what I say is still taken as representation for all trans people.

I think that's why after a while I started talking more about being a young trans woman of color who grew up poor in Honolulu. That way people can't say that my experience is representative of anyone else's because I don't think that many people have that specific experience. What I've learned, even with writing, is that the more specific you are, the more universal it becomes.

It becomes this thing where it's like, "Oh, wow, you talk about child sexual abuse," or "You talk about sex work as a teenager." Your story resonates with a lot more people the more specific and honest and truthful you are. That's why I wanted to key back in on just claiming the identity of writer, because when I stand firmly in that identity, it is my craft and my work and my stories that stand before me and that lead the way, and not so much this idea of being this activist or this advocate who is out there representing all these people. Instead, it's the story that tends to then represent or shed light on people whose voices aren't heard.

**Nia:** Do you feel a lot of pressure because you are seen as a role model? It seems like you're on a pedestal that would be very easy to fall off of.

**Janet:** Yeah. I always think about Toni Morrison. I think about her career and how big critics told her—this was said in a review of her first book, *The Bluest Eye*—that she had the potential to become a serious American writer when she wrote "beyond the Black experience." This was in a major review of her book, and it's like, "Oh, wow." [*laughter*] I think that if you're a person of color and you write about people-of-color issues, then that's all you become known for.

As a young trans woman of color who's writing about young-trans-women-of-color issues, I cannot escape the fact that my identity will lead the way to my work. That is often a big battle—that people will see the story of my life as more important than the craft that it took to make that story come to life and communicate it in a way that makes someone feel entertained and also informs them of a different kind of human experience.

In conversations, bell hooks has told me, "You just have to own it, baby girl"—that the trans intersection and trans identity are going to lead the way, that people are going to see that I have this fantastical, inspirational story, and they're not really going to recognize the craft that it took to tell that story. She goes, "Your identity is going to lead the way before your work," but she also said the work would stand the test of time and that I just have to have faith in that. That has given me strength, hearing that from someone else who's been there and who understands this—having been a Black feminist critic and theorist—that her Blackness, that her Black woman-ness is what leads the way before people actually talk about the ideas she writes about and the way that she writes them.

**Nia:** Do you think that your journalism background and experience in higher education has helped prepare you for what you're doing now?

**Janet:** Oh, *yeah*. My entire career has been in media, so I know how a journalist thinks. When a journalist comes to me for a story, I know that I need to give them something that they can use as a great headline or a pull-quote or something like that. [*laughter*] I know how to be a good interviewee and that helps a lot with being seen and heard and being impactful in an interview. My education has helped because it credentialized me. I'm a mixed-race trans woman who has a master's degree and that is rare. If we're being specific, in this anti-Black world, I'm a Black woman, period, who has a master's degree.

I know that the credentials have helped. Having a master's from NYU helped me get my job at People.com and helped me get all these internships where I got to meet all these amazing people and work with editors and make connections. Without People.com, the *Marie Claire* piece would have never happened. All of it has been for a grander purpose. I think that it's all been set up for the launch of and the sharing of my book, which I know is going to be a major moment. For me, it's not so much about trying to get my book to be mainstream—it's about trying to get it to audiences that might not touch it normally. The ones who don't follow me on Twitter are the ones I'm trying to get to, so that when they encounter trans people—specifically young trans women—they don't look at them in disgust. They'll look at them in a different kind of way because my story is then projected onto those trans people.

**Nia:** When you talk about your career history, it sort of sounds like you went to school and then you got a job at *InStyle* and got a job at *People* and then you became an editor and then you came out in *Marie Claire* and now you have a book and you're all over TV. I feel like there must be something missing from that version of the story. It's obviously hard work that got you to all of those different places, but making a name for yourself as a writer is really hard. I'm curious about whether you were ever at the point where I am now, trying really hard to get your name out there and figuring out how to monetize what it is that you have to offer. You sort of briefly mentioned that year between the *Marie Claire* piece coming out and when you started getting paying speaking gigs. What was that year like?

**Janet:** That year was a transitional year. That first year, I didn't know that speaking was something that I could monetize. A lot of the places that I ended up speaking at early on were for a lot of trans youth events and causes. My first speaking gig that I got paid pretty well for was a commencement address at the University of Southern California [USC], for their Lavender Commencement Celebration. That was my first big speech. My boyfriend recorded it and put a snippet of it online, which was a great reel for me to have. People could see that I could speak and hold a crowd and tell a moving story.

At the end of the day, it's about storytelling. People are attracted to great stories, and they will want to hear a great story over and over and over again. I think that my story is a great story that I've been able to use to color experiences and to contextualize other pressing issues. I use a lot of my personal experiences to color and make those issues feel more immediate for people, so people can see me as my sixteen-year-old self on Trans Day of Remembrance, going on my first date with a guy who doesn't know I'm trans. Telling that story makes it more real on the level of "Oh, wow, now I can see why a lot of trans women—young trans women—end up facing abuse through intimate partner violence."

I was a salaried employee when I worked for *People*. I was taken care of. I was *comfortable*. I had a job that was coveted. It was hard getting to that job. I did other internships, too. I had a paid internship at *Playboy Magazine*—I was an editorial intern there. I even did fashion closet work at *InStyle* until I went into an editorial position there.

**Nia:** What is "fashion closet work"?

**Janet:** Fashion magazines, they call for a lot of clothes to come in, so they get shipped in—in boxes or in bags from fashion studios in New York City, or beyond New York City, from warehouses. When that stuff comes in and needs to be inventoried and taken out of the boxes, all of the pieces need to be catalogued, so someone does that job, and it tends to be the intern.

**Nia:** Okay, so it's a literal closet that you're talking about?

**Janet:** Yes. There's a sea of interns who are packing and shipping things. Once the editors are done with the clothes, you put them back into their original packaging and into a box. You're boxing up boxes, putting labels on them, and giving them to the messenger guys who then send them out. Eight hours a day, you're like a factory worker. That's what your internship is. The girls who *love* fashion do this like *die-hard*. They love it. They love it because they know it's a step forward. I fucking *hated* it. It was the worst.

That transitional year, I was waiting for a book deal and I continued to write essays on my website and beyond. I continued my social media presence. I was growing an audience. That year was about building. My work is still about building those relationships with people on social media, through Facebook and Twitter and Tumblr. Once I got the book deal, it enabled me to leave my job. I got a speaking agent once I got the book deal—someone who helped me set up my book tour, but also someone who was going to help me to begin monetizing my speaking at colleges. But a lot of my speaking gigs came through word of mouth. I did something good at USC, it went online, people saw it, and other colleges were like, "Let's start booking Janet for the fall semester!"

The majority of my speaking events I got because of my relationships on social media. It was all through other young people who were attracted to my story, to things that I wrote—like the piece that I wrote about coming out to Aaron, my boyfriend. People who were connected to me and enjoyed my commentary were like, "We should bring her, we should invite her to speak!" When they organize, my name is in their mouths. They're the ones who are bringing me to colleges. It's all through young people, through social media.

**Nia:** Now that you've written your first book, which has been the dream for such a long time, what do you want to do next?

**Janet:** Oh, my. I'd like to write more books. I don't know what those books look like yet. I know there's definitely one about my young womanhood, because I think this book [*Redefining Realness*] is a lot about my girlhood and my path to becoming a woman. I haven't really written extensively on what it is to be a young woman in this culture, through the lens of the experience of a trans woman of color. I think that's a book, but I think it's a book that I probably won't be ready to write until three to five years from now. I do want to write another book soon and I don't know yet what it would be about.

Maybe about beauty culture, how I came to beauty and self-image and self-love and all of that stuff, because it's weird that people perceive me as pretty. People will come up to me and be like, "Oh my god!" Do you know what I mean? Like, they'll just be stunned and there'll be this weird interaction, because beauty is a social experience, but it's also a personal experience. My relationship with myself is not looking at myself and being like, "Oh my god, I'm so pretty!"

**Nia:** [*laughter*]

**Janet:** Do you know what I mean? I still remember when I didn't feel that way about myself and I am still struggling with certain things. Like, now I know I have it goin' on. Now I can stand in that. In the last couple years, I've been like, "Yes. I'm an attractive, smart, hard-working woman. This is me." I've been able to stand in that. It took a long time to get there, but people only see what you show them, right?

**Nia:** Can I ask you about your internship at *Playboy*? It sounds like it might be an interesting story.

**Janet:** [*laughter*] It actually is not! In New York City, it was only the editorial staff—a lot of the photography stuff happened in Chicago and LA. I saw the covers, I saw the inside spreads and the make-readies for the pages and the layout and stuff, but they weren't something I was shocked by. I'm not shocked by the naked body or pornography. I saw these women as choosing to bare their bodies in this prestigious men's magazine—for the male gaze, of course, but I didn't see it from a perspective of like, "Oh, poor innocent girls who are having to be objectified!" It *is* a little weird that you see these naked bodies in a place of work, like…

**Nia:** [*laughter*]

**Janet:** Like, it's next to a Truman Capote short story! Or a Joan Didion story! Or a piece from a short story writer no one knows about! They actually have a literary history at *Playboy*. That's why it was one of the most fulfilling editorial experiences. They let me write things. I was a freelancer for them after I was an intern there. I wrote interview pieces for them—short little things like front-of-the-book, back-of-the-book stuff, but it was a great experience.

It was a bunch of dorks. There's a tech guy who writes about all the new gadgets, a movie reviewer, and a short literary editor—this woman who's been editing short stories forever. These people are in their little silos, so it's like you're just working with editors who have these very specific tasks.

I did a lot of research for this guy who had a sex advice column, but it was more like a practical sex advice column. He was doing a science-focused series on men and sexuality from boyhood to adulthood. I was doing a lot of research for him, looking through academic journals and stuff—so that was my work at *Playboy*.

**Nia:** [*laughter*]

**Janet:** You know, like, I didn't see Hugh Hefner, I didn't get to go to the Playboy Mansion… [*laughter*]

**Nia:** What do you wish people would ask you? Is there something about your work that you feel like you never get to talk about?

**Janet:** I think process is something people don't often ask about. I think people like to buy into the idea that you came out of nowhere and are just super successful. I mean, that's what will happen and will get erased with my book. The book will be successful and people will say, "Boom, see, it just happened!" But people aren't interested in the process of what that actually looked like, right? What does it mean to come to a place where there are thirty to fifty thousand people following you on social media, to have that kind of a presence as someone who doesn't necessarily have a mainstream, everyday presence in people's lives? I'm supposedly just this writer trans girl, you know what I mean? Like how does that actually happen? What's the process of that?

People aren't interested in the process because we're in a fame- and success-minded culture. They just want to know the "after," not the "during," right? People don't ask about the process. If *Redefining Realness* is a bestseller, if it shoots up on *The New York Times* bestseller list, then the media will pay attention. They will write me as this underdog who came out of nowhere and they will write my success as being unlike any other thing that could happen and then I'll become a media darling, right? But no one will talk about the process it took to get to that.

Transcribed by Weily Lang

## Nia King
*This interview was conducted via email.*

**Co-editors Jessica Glennon-Zukoff and Terra Mikalson:** You have created an archive of advice from queer artists of color on making it as an artist—what advice-gems stand out in your mind?

**Nia King:** One piece of advice that's come up a lot on the podcast is "Don't work for free." I think monetizing your work is one of the hardest things about being an artist because everyone wants art, but nobody wants to pay for it. Folks feel like artists should be happy to work for "exposure," but exposure is not going to pay your rent or put food in your fridge. It seems to me like it's not *as* hard to start getting more paid gigs and get paid at higher rates as it is to make that initial jump from unpaid artist to paid artist.

When Virgie Tovar first told me that she saw herself as part of a movement demanding payment for artists, I thought that was kind of extreme—or maybe unfair to artists who might really need the exposure. But now I realize how much creative labor—art-making—is devalued in our society. Queer art activists of color are never going to be able to make a living doing our art if we don't demand payment for it. Art adds value to people's lives and thus artists should be able to support themselves making it, instead of having to sell their labor, body, or soul to others in order to keep creating.

**Terra:** Can you talk a little bit about the significance of artist interview portions that are not strictly about identity, art, or politics, but rather about things like Ryka Aoki's chemistry job?

**Nia:** I like to try and ask questions that I think people haven't been asked before. Ryka is known as a speaker and a writer, but obviously her work has been influenced by more than just her current occupations or her identity. I found out that Ryka was also a chemist and a martial arts master—those are things that influence her work even if they don't always make it into her bio. I think it makes the artists feel respected when I ask non-obvious questions because they get to be seen as a whole, multifaceted person, rather than someone whose value is determined just based on the things they create. I'd also like to think that these kinds of questions make my interviews unique.

When people from marginalized communities are interviewed, they're often asked questions about being an Other, which then makes them *feel* like an Other and that can push people into a more defensive, explanatory mode. I try to ask about experiences that shape people and make them who they are, beyond just their identities as marginalized people. I think feeling wholly seen allows people to feel safer opening up more, so we get to move beyond the 101-level-type questions.

Another thing I hate that I feel like I see on talk shows a lot is when interviewers seem to really want to focus on not only what makes the subject *different* but also on what makes their life *hard*. Yosimar Reyes and Fabian Romero both talk in their interviews about other people's perverse fascination with their hardships. There were times where guests opened up about things that seemed like they would be really hard to talk about—surviving homelessness, cancer, rape—and instead of going deeper, I often backed away or made a conscious effort to bring the focus of the conversation back to the artist's work. I didn't want to reopen wounds for folks and then just abandon them with their pain when the interview was over.

**Jessica:** What do *you* like to be asked about?

**Nia:** I like talking about the ethics of art activism because it's something I think about and struggle with a lot. It feels like a big responsibility to be the holder of people's stories and to figure out what to do with them. I've had people come out to me as sex workers and survivors during interviews, which I was not expecting. I've had people say things that I thought were going to make them look bad or damage their reputation and then I had to ask myself, "Do I cut it? Do I keep it? Is my obligation to protect the artists, potentially even from themselves, or to protect the community from them if they really do hold these oppressive beliefs they seem to be espousing?"

It's so easy for things to be taken out of context. Sometimes, someone says something and I think, "That sounds really bad and I know you didn't mean it that way," but I don't know if I can trust the audience to give them that benefit of the doubt. Those are the kinds of things I struggle with and that I try to talk about with other interviewers to figure out how they deal with those types of issues. I still feel really new at this.

**Jessica and Terra:** What has been the most surprising piece of feedback you've gotten about the podcast?

**Nia:** After my first interview, I asked Virgie Tovar, who worked in radio for years, if she had any interview tips for me. She said I should argue with the guests more. I was really surprised by it at the time. In my head, I was like, "The guest is God. Who am *I* to argue with *them*?"

As I've gotten more comfortable interviewing, I've also gotten more comfortable challenging guests when they say something that comes across as a problematic generalization or hyperbole. I don't try to attack my guests, but I think sometimes being asked to defend your position forces you to clarify your thoughts and make sure what you're saying is what you mean and actually makes sense.

**Jessica and Terra:** What's your philosophy for how much of yourself to put into interviews?

**Nia:** In the beginning, I was really shy and really bad about speaking up—I got a lot of complaints that I was inaudible on the podcast, actually. I wanted so badly for it to be all about the guest that I didn't even mic myself! I still try not to make it too much about me, but sometimes talking about myself first allows me to articulate a question that's not fully fleshed out yet. It also gives the guest something to relate to and work off of.

**Terra:** You learned about anti-oppressive research methods as an undergraduate at Mills College in the Ethnic Studies Department. Have the methodologies you learned at Mills, or studied on your own since graduating, influenced how you conduct interviews?

**Nia:** Definitely. I think the most important thing I've learned is that trust is *the* most important thing in an interview. I also learned that the interviewer has a responsibility to take care of the interviewee emotionally, to not just use them for information. That idea is really emphasized in the feminist and disability justice research methodologies I studied at Mills.

I also learned the importance of not asking leading questions. If your questions are laden with value judgments, the interviewee will get defensive and closed-off. I don't want guests to feel bullied into giving a certain answer. The interviews I feel least happy with are the ones where I feel like I came in with an agenda, even when the agenda was fairly vague, like "I want to talk about comedy" or someone's experience in the military or current events.

Letting the conversation go where it goes organically tends to yield much better, more interesting results.

**Jessica and Terra:** If you could stop one question from being asked of queer people of color ever again, what would it be?

**Nia:** "What's it like being X?" X could be any identity-marker—queer, trans, Black, Asian, disabled...I recently read an interview where Aziz Ansari mentioned how much he hates being asked "What's it like being an Indian American comedian?" and Amy Poehler has also complained publicly many times about being asked "What's it like being a woman in comedy?" These kinds of questions are so basic that asking them makes it really hard to get to information that both the artist and the audience would probably find much more interesting.

I think that any question someone gets over and over they're going to have a canned answer for, and I don't want guests going on autopilot and waiting for the interview to be over. I want to make a genuine connection with them and find out what makes them tick. It's easier to do that when you treat them like a human rather than a spectacle.

**Jessica and Terra:** Do you feel you've grown as an interviewer as the podcast has developed?

**Nia:** I hope so! When I did my first interview with Virgie Tovar, I was really nervous and stuck strictly to the script. When I interviewed Kortney Ryan Ziegler, I overcompensated, got completely away from my prepared questions, and the interview ended up being three hours long. I've figured out how to keep the interviews to approximately one hour but also how to improvise. It can be challenging to think up questions while you are listening, but I think asking follow-up questions based on what someone has just said makes them feel listened to and also allows the conversation to go organically to a more interesting place than it might have otherwise.

**Jessica:** A theme I've noticed in these interviews is a kind of derision for call-out culture. What, in your mind, is call-out culture? Do you think the call-out has developed a bad reputation widely?

**Nia:** Call-out culture is the idea that we should publicly shame people who behave in oppressive ways, particularly on the Internet. I think when you're feeling oppressed, intimidated, or silenced, calling someone out online can seem like a really appealing option. Unfortunately, there are a lot of people who know how to use social justice language to obfuscate their own oppressive behavior, and those people often end up being those doing the calling out.

At its worst, call-out culture, particularly online, represents the merger of social justice culture and trolling. By the time you've been called out for something publicly, your reputation is already damaged and anything you say in your own defense becomes suspect, colored by the idea that you are a bad person just trying to cover up or make excuses for bad behavior.

I do think the call-out has developed a bad reputation, and rightfully so. I don't want to say I think we need to have more "compassion" for each other, because I think that approach often benefits the people who are oppressing others and is implemented at the expense of the people they are hurting. As people who care about social justice, we tend to feel obligated to take negative feedback very seriously when it's couched in social justice terms. I think we need to be more aware of the fact that there are people who pervert the language of social justice to portray themselves as victims when they are actually the ones perpetrating violence and oppressive behavior against other marginalized people.

**Jessica and Terra:** You are a writer, instructor, filmmaker, cartoonist, and podcast host, not to mention a badass researcher. What approaches do you take to promoting yourself and your work? Also, why are you so awesome?

**Nia:** Aww, thanks, you guys! I blame my parents.

I promote my work and myself as much as I am able and it's pretty exhausting. Building a website has probably been the most useful thing for my professional career. When I cold-call artists asking to interview them, they can look at my site and they usually decide I seem legit. I think that would be less true if the only places I could send them to learn more about me were my Facebook, Twitter, or Tumblr. That said, I do use all three of those social media platforms a lot to promote my work, especially Twitter.

**Jessica and Terra:** We know that you identify not-so-secretly as a homebody and introvert. Do you feel like that affects your professional and creative pursuits?

**Nia:** Being a homebody is good for hunkering down and getting work done. It's not so good for networking, but I prefer to talk to people one-on-one anyway, as opposed to in big group settings. I'm not someone who can go to things just to schmooze because the pressure to meet and charm people is too great. Sometimes, if I'm at a performance, I'll approach the performer after the show and see if they want to come on the podcast. Sometimes, if I'm too shy to talk to someone in person, I'll tweet at them to see if they want to come on the show. It helps if you open with a compliment.

I think, more than being a homebody and introvert, what hurts my professional and creative pursuits is struggling with depression. I think people who follow me on social media can tell that I work really hard and am constantly producing new stuff, but I feel like I could get a lot more done if I had more energy. Both my depression and my chronic pain make it so that I have to spend a lot of time recuperating from life when I could hypothetically be creating work. I'm really trying to work through my internalized ableism, though, and be proud of what I *do* get done, instead of ashamed about how much I had hoped to accomplish but didn't.

**Jessica and Terra:** What is your hope for this book?

**Nia:** I really want QTPOC art activism to become a flourishing field of research and study, which I hope will create more institutional and economic support for marginalized artists to keep doing what they do. A lot of QTPOC cultural institutions are not documented—you only find out about them through word of mouth or by being in the right place at the right time—and they're often very short-lived because people don't have the resources to sustain them.

I wanted to create this book so that the work of these amazing artists who have influenced me will not seem like a flash in the pan if they eventually burn out or go broke and have to stop creating. I want there to be a record of their wisdom and their influence and their greatness that will inspire others to create as well. I really do believe that QTPOC art activism saves lives, and this book is just one of my many efforts to show how and why.

**Jessica and Terra:** What advice would you personally give to other queer artists of color on making it as an artist?

**Nia:** Firstly, don't compromise your vision to make your art more marketable to a community that is not your own.
Secondly, find community with other artists who are like you and who get what you're trying to do. If you're trying to make work about race or gender or sexuality in a class with a bunch of straight white guys, there's a chance you might get good feedback, but a lot of times, you're going to encounter resistance and an inability to engage with whatever it is you're presenting. Then, the feedback you're getting there might not be as useful as feedback you might get from other people who have personal experience with the issues you're trying to examine in your work.

Lastly, don't be afraid of failure, or at least don't let it hold you back. A part of why you're at a disadvantage as a queer or trans person of color is that you're queer or trans and of color, but another reason is that people who have privilege often don't let the fact that they don't know what they're talking about stop them from talking. They don't let the fact that they don't know what they're doing stop them from doing stuff.

Doing stuff is how you learn and how you get exposure, so overcoming fear of failure is really important if you want to become successful as an artist. I think you have to operate with the faith that you *will* get a second chance if you mess up, whether or not you really believe that's true. If you don't at least believe on some level that it's okay to make mistakes and that you will eventually get another chance, it's hard to get anywhere.

## Artist Bios

**Toi Scott** is a visionary community organizer, artivist, medicine maker, spiritual activist and ordinary superhero. Toi believes in co-creating healing and transformation within multiple, intersecting communities by working toward racial and gender justice and the eradication of oppression within the economic, food, and health care systems. Toi has written zines, resource guides, and plays including *Notes from an Afro-Genderqueer*, *Philosophactivism*, *Queering Herbalism*, *Herbal Freedom School*, and *Resistencia: Sangre*. Learn more at: http://www.afrogenderqueer.com.

**Ryka Aoki** has been honored by the California State Senate for "extraordinary commitment to free speech and artistic expression, as well as the visibility and well-being of transgender people." Her collection *Seasonal Velocities* was a finalist for a 2013 Lambda Literary Award in Transgender Nonfiction. Ryka also appears in *Gender Outlaws: The Next Generation, Transfeminist Perspectives,* and *The Collection*. Her novel, *He Mele a Hilo,* was be published by Topside Signature Press in spring 2014. She is a professor of English at Santa Monica College and of Gender Studies at Antioch University. www.rykaryka.com

**Van Binfa** is a queer, Chilean trans activist who works within the Chicago Latin@ community. Van and Ivonne Canellada founded Soy Quien Soy, a trans empowerment collective based in Pilsen, which is now an online resource page. Van has served on several boards and done the activist gig for a few years. He is passionate about the representation of trans people of color within queer organizations. In addition to being a writer and avid *Supernatural* fan, Van is also an artist. His art emphasizes the resilience of trans people of color. Van believes in the individual, everyday acts of activism.

**Micia Mosely, PhD,** was praised by newyorktheatre.com as "smart, timely and also downright hilarious." This comedian and educator earned her PhD in education from U.C. Berkeley and keeps audiences learning and laughing in a variety of contexts and venues. Mosely's one-woman show *Where My Girls At?* (an off-Broadway comedy about Black lesbians) was nominated for a New York Innovative Theatre Award (Best Solo Performance). She performs stand-up comedy and teaches at U.C. Berkeley & UMass Boston. www.miciamosely.com

**Yosimar Reyes** is a nationally-acclaimed poet based out of San Jose, CA. He holds the title for the 2005 as well as the 2006 South Bay Teen Grand SLAM Champion. He has also been featured in the documentary *2nd Verse: the Rebirth of Poetry* (2ndversefilm.com) and published in *Mariposas: A Modern Anthology of Queer Latino Poetry* (Floricanto Press). When he is not rocking the stage with his diva attitude, you can catch Yosimar waiting for the bus and sharing PALABRA with his abuelita, always breaking it down hood and speaking from a community spirit. He currently lives in East Side San Jose.

**Kortney Ryan Ziegler** is an entrepreneur, writer, artist, and loving human being.

**Lovemme "Love" Corazón** es una bruja, a magical gurl dropout, a wannabe xingona, a genderescent divinity, and a political trans woman of color. She is a poet, a mixed media artist, and the author of *Trauma Queen*. She aspires to create films centered on queer and trans people of color. vivalaluna.com

**Fabian Romero** is a Queer Chicano writer. They co-founded several writing and performance groups including Hijas de Su Madre, Las Mamalogues and Mixed Messages: Stories by People of Color. Their work can be found in *Troubling the Line: Trans and Genderqueer Poetry and Poetics,* and in the near future in *To The Exclusion of All Others: Queers Questioning Gay Marriage.* Fabian was born in Michoacán, Mexico and came to North America when they were seven years old. Since 2007, they have performed throughout North America. They are pursuing a BA at Evergreen State College with a focus in creative writing.

**Magnoliah Black** (a.k.a. Irene McCalphin) is a New Orleans native and Bay Area transplant. She is a storyteller who promotes body love and diversity through the mediums of vocal performance, dance, burlesque, writing and public speaking. She performs both as a soloist and as a core member of the internationally-traveled and award-winning Rubenesque Burlesque. You can find her at rubenesqueburlesque.com and at misadventuresofanungratefulfatbitch.com.

**Kiam Marcelo Junio** is a multidisciplinary artist living in Chicago. They work in multiple media, including photography, video, printmaking, installation, burlesque, and performance art. His research and artwork center around queer identities, the Filipino American diaspora, post-colonialist Asian American tropes and stereotypes, and military and civilian power dynamics. Jerry Blossom is Kiam's performative alter-ego, a genderqueer Filipino femme-presenting persona who hails from an alternate post-queer, post-colonialist utopia. Kiam served seven years in the US Navy. They were born in the Philippines and have lived in the US, Japan, and Spain. They are also a registered yoga teacher.

**DADDIE$ PLA$TIK** is a multimedia performance project featuring the sounds and visuals of three Bay Area based artists: Tyler Holmes, San Cha, & Vain Hein...as well as a slew of other collaborators. **Miss Persia** is a San Francisco-based drag queen.

**Virgie Tovar**, MA, is an author, activist and one of the nation's leading experts and lecturers on fat discrimination and body image. She is the editor of *Hot & Heavy: Fierce Fat Girls on Life, Love & Fashion* (Seal Press, November 2012). Virgie has been featured by *MTV*, *Al Jazeera*, the *San Francisco Chronicle*, *NPR*, *Huffington Post*, *Bust Magazine*, *Jezebel*, and *XOJane*, as well as on *Women's Entertainment Television* and *The Ricki Lake Show*. Find her online at virgietovar.com.

**Julio Salgado** is a queer Mexican-born artist who grew up in Long Beach, California. Salgado uses his art to empower undocumented and queer people by helping tell their stories through powerful images, which help put a human face to the issue.

**Nick Hadikwa Mwaluko** was born in Tanzania and raised mostly in neighboring Kenya and other East and Central African countries. Nick would like to thank Nia King for this great opportunity. Set in a rural Kenyan village, Nick's book *Waafrika* is a love story between a trans-African from the Luo tribe and an American formerly with the Peace Corps. Copies of *Waafrika* are available online at Amazon.com, at Marcus Bookstore in Oakland, and by emailing Nick at tanzanianexport@gmail.com.

**Leah Lakshmi Piepzna-Samarasinha** is a queer disabled Sri Lankan cis femme writer, performer, organizer and badass visionary healer. The author of the Lambda Award-winning *Love Cake* and *Consensual Genocide* and co-editor of *The Revolution Starts At Home*. Her work has appeared in the anthologies such as *Undoing Border Imperialism, Yes Means Yes, Colonize This, Without a Net,* and *A Girl's Guide to Taking Over The World*. She co-founded Mangos With Chili and Toronto's Asian Arts Freedom School and is a lead artist with Sins Invalid.

**Janet Mock** is the author of *Redefining Realness* and founder of #girlslikeus, a movement for trans women living visibly. Janet is a board member at the Arcus Foundation, has been recognized by the Sylvia Rivera Law Project, the Anti-Violence Project, and the Center for American Progress, and has been featured in the HBO documentary *The OUT List* and on MSNBC's *Melissa Harris-Perry*. She attended her hometown college, the University of Hawaii, earned her MA in journalism from NYU, and worked as an editor at People.com. She lives and writes in New York City.

# Editor Bios

**Jessica Glennon-Zukoff** is a white lower/working-class queer femme who graduated from Mills College with a BA in Women's, Gender, and Sexuality Studies (WGSS) and English Literature. She wrote her undergraduate English thesis on spaces for queerness paradoxically created by heteropatriarchy in Christina Rossetti's "Goblin Market" and her WGSS thesis on what happens when Evangelical Christian kids realize they're queer (she should know). When she's not daydreaming about what femmes of all genders from centuries past might have been up to, she loves reading work from fields of fat studies, disability studies, and work on inter-class relationships, especially through a queer-femme lens.

**Terra Mikalson** graduated from Mills College with a BA in Ethnic Studies. Ze is passionate about queer and trans mental health and building queer, radical, anti-Zionist Jewish community. Some of Terra's self-care practices include creating fabulous, highly-intentional outfits; dancing; scrolling through social justice Tumblr blogs; and making up songs such as "Cry Your Cis Tears," sung to the tune of "Cool Rider" from *Grease 2*. Ze also enjoys jigsaw puzzles and dark chocolate.

**Nia King** is a queer mixed Black art activist from Boston living in Oakland, California. Her writing has been published in *Women and Performance: A Journal of Feminist Theory*, *Zines in Third Space: Radical Cooperation and Borderlands Rhetoric*, and *make/shift* magazine. Her comics have been featured in *Colorlines*, *Interrupt Mag*, and in the Ladydrawers exhibition "Sex. Money. Race. Gender." Her film, *The Craigslist Chronicles*, has screened at the National Queer Arts Festival, York University, the University of Toronto, and NYU. Get in touch at niaking@zoho.com, ArtActivistNia.com, or @ArtActivistNia on Twitter.

## Acknowledgements

José Esteban Muñoz and Mangos with Chili have made incredible contributions to the field of QTPOC art activism. This book is built largely upon their work.

I'd like to thank my co-editors Jessica Glennon-Zukoff and Terra Mikalson for their tireless work on this book, the transcribers for making the podcast accessible to deaf and hard-of-hearing audiences, my mom and Myles for their moral support, Channing Kennedy and Micia Mosely for their guidance, Nico Vitti (nicovitti.com) and Tali Weinberg (taliweinberg.com) for their graphic design work, Sapna Kumar (sapna-kumar.com) for proofreading, and all the artists who have been on the podcast for trusting me with their stories.

This book is a DIY labor of love. All of the money needed to self-publish this book—to pay the artists, editors, graphic designer, etc.—was raised online through Indiegogo. Thank you to all of the donors for believing in this project and for making it possible.

## Donors:

A.J. Bryce
Abigail Bunyan
Alice Eastman
Amanda Ching
Amanda Vodola
Amber Nash
Amelia Hooper
Amirah Mizrahi
Andrea Merrill
Brittany Breithaupt
C. Young
Canela Jaramillo
Carolyn Gretton
Carolyn Wysinger
Carrie Tilton-Jones

Cathy Camper
Celeste Chan
Channing Kennedy
Christian Keeve
Claire Black
Claudia Leung
Claudius-Maximus T. Humboldt
Colin K. Donovan
Cory Watson
Creatrix Tiara
Daniel P. McCall
Deborah Manigault
E. Adiakpan
Emily Aaron
Eric Ginsburg

Franny Howes
H. Melton
Hannah Assebe
Heather Jarvis
Isabelle Jagninski
Jack Elliott
Jaime-Jin
Jamie Varriale
Jen-Mei Wu
Jess Brooke
Joyce Hatton
Kandee Lewis
Kelly Costello
Kerri Lynne Thorp
Kyem Brown
Laura Barsigian
Lauren Smith
Lauren Soldano
Lex Non Scripta
Lily Hoffman-Andrews
Lily Pepper
Lilyanne
Linda Nguyen
Lisa Weems
Loren Barry
Lucy Corona
Maisha Johnson
Maranda Elizabeth
Mariana Lui
Mark Williams
Megan Derr
Michael Floyd
Michele Glennon
Michelle Castor
Michelle L. Pettis
Michelle W.
Mimi Thi Nguyen
Monika Eggers
Muna Mire
Natalie Gee
Nicole M. Vermeer
Nimmy Abiaka
Nora Berenstain
Quirk Goodman
Rachel Miranda Wedig
Raisa Slutsky-Moore

Robert Lopez
Rose Murphree Gamble
Rose Robertson
Rowen Lohmann
Ryka Aoki
Samantha Press
Sara Rosa Espi
Sarah Christine Meyers
Sarah Kelly
Shane Patrick Boyle
Shannon Perez-Darby
Shawna Virago
Steve Siwy
Talcott Broadhead
Tali Weinberg
Tanaya Thomas
Tiffany Marceaux McCulley
Tina Vasquez
Ty C.
Vanessa Lewis
Voula O'Grady
Weily Lang
Weyam Ghadbian

Made in the USA
San Bernardino, CA
07 August 2018